All-Star 2

Linda Lee

Kristin Sherman ★ **Stephen Sloan**

Grace Tanaka ★ **Shirley Velasco**

D1708034

All-Star 2 1st Edition

Published by McGraw-Hill ESL/ELT, a business unit of The McGraw-Hill Companies, Inc. 1221 Avenue of the Americas, New York, NY 10020. Copyright © 2005 by The McGraw-Hill Companies, Inc. All rights reserved. No part of this publication may be reproduced or distributed in any form or by any means, or stored in a database or retrieval system, without the prior written consent of The McGraw-Hill Companies, Inc., including, but not limited to, in any network or other electronic storage or transmission, or broadcast for distance learning.

ISBN-13: 978-0-07-284674-4 (Student Book)
ISBN-10: 0-07-284674-7
6 7 8 9 10 QPD 09 08 07 06

ISBN-13: 978-0-07-304873-4 (Student book with Audio Highlights)
ISBN-10: 0-07-304873-9
8 9 10 QPD 09 08 07 06

Editorial director Tina B. Carver
Executive editor Erik Gundersen
Director of sales and marketing Thomas P. Dare
Developmental editors Jennifer Monaghan, Mari Vargo
Editorial assistant David Averbach
Production manager Juanita Thompson
Interior designer Wee Design Group
Cover designer Wee Design Group
Illustrators Anna Divito, Andrew Lange, NETS/Carlos Sanchis, Blanche Sims, Chris Winn
Photo Research NETS
Photo Credits
   All photos courtesy of Getty Images Royalty-Free collection with the exception of the following: page 14 © Spencer Grant/PhotoEdit; page 30 © Tony Freeman/PhotoEdit; page 58 © Wally McNamee/CORBIS; page 58 © Visser Robert/CORBIS; page 62 © Chuck Savage/CORBIS; page 63 © Keith Dannemiller/CORBIS; page 72 © Jose Luis Pelaez, Inc./CORBIS; page 73 © David Young-Wolff/PhotoEdit; page 73 © Amy Etra/PhotoEdit; page 79 © Dennis MacDonald/PhotoEdit; page 91 © AJA Productions/Getty Images; page 110 and 111 © David Averbach.

The McGraw·Hill Companies

ACKNOWLEDGEMENTS

The authors and publisher would like to thank the following individuals who reviewed the *All-Star* program at various stages of development and whose comments, reviews, and field-testing were instrumental in helping us shape the series:

Carol Antunano • The English Center; Miami, FL

Feliciano Atienza • YMCA Elesair Project; New York, NY

Nancy Baxer • Lutheran Social Ministries of New Jersey Refugee Resettlement Program; Trenton, NJ

Jeffrey P. Bright • Albany Park Community Center; Chicago, IL

Enzo Caserta • Miami Palmetto Adult Education Center; Miami, FL

Allison Freiman • YMCA Elesair Project; New York, NY

Susan Gaer • Santa Ana College School of Continuing Education; Santa Ana, CA

Toni Galaviz • Reseda Community Adult School; Reseda, CA

Maria Hegarty • SCALE; Somerville, MA

Virginia Hernandez • Miami Palmetto Adult Education Center; Miami, FL

Giang Hoang • Evans Community Adult School; Los Angeles, CA

Edwina Hoffman • Miami-Dade County Adult Schools; Miami, FL

Ionela Istrate • YMCA of Greater Boston International Learning Center; Boston, MA

Janice Jensen • Santa Ana College School of Continuing Education; Santa Ana, CA

Jan Jerrell • San Diego Community College District; San Diego, CA

Margaret Kirkpatrick • Berkeley Adult School; Berkeley, CA

LaRanda Marr • Oakland Unified School District; Office of Adult Education; Oakland, CA

Patricia Mooney-Gonzalez • New York State Department of Education; Albany, NY

Paula Orias • Piper Community School; Broward County Public Schools; Sunrise, FL

Linda O'Roke • City College of San Francisco; San Francisco, CA

Betsy Parrish • Hamline University; St. Paul, MN

Mary Pierce • Xavier Adult School; New York, NY

Marta Pitt • Lindsey Hopkins Technical Education Center; Miami, FL

Donna Price-Machado • San Diego Community College District; San Diego, CA

Sylvia Ramirez • Community Learning Center • MiraCosta College; Oceanside, CA

Inna Reydel • YMCA of Greater Boston International Learning Center; Boston, MA

Leslie Shimazaki • San Diego Community College District; San Diego, CA

Betty Stone • SCALE; Somerville, MA

Theresa Suslov • SCALE; Somerville, MA

Dave VanLew • Simi Valley Adult & Career Institute; Simi Valley, CA

Scope and Sequence

	Life Skills				
Unit	**Listening and Speaking**	**Reading and Writing**	**Critical Thinking**	**Vocabulary**	**Grammar**
Pre-Unit **Getting Started** *page 2*	• Introduce yourself • Use useful expressions • Follow and give classroom instructions			• Introductions • Useful expressions • Classroom instructions	
1 **Describing People** *page 4*	• Exchange personal information • Describe people • Greet a friend • Make introductions **Pronunciation Focus:** Vowel sounds in *slip* and *sleep*	• Read and interpret personal documents (birth certificate, driver's license, diploma) • Read a website for specific information • Read and write bio poems • Write about likes and dislikes • Interpret personal information forms • Complete a driver's license application	• Interpret information • Reason	• Personal information (name, address, date of birth) • Physical descriptions • Moods and emotions	• Present tense statements: regular verbs and *have* • Present tense negative statements • *Yes/no* questions with *do* or *does* **Spotlight:** Simple present statements; *yes/no* questions with the simple present
2 **Going Places** *page 20*	• Ask about places in the community • Ask for and give directions • Ask for information at a train station **Pronunciation Focus:** *S* versus *Z*	• Read a map • Read a train schedule • Read a telephone directory • Read and evaluate a website **Spotlight:** Personal letters; envelopes	• Interpret a map • Make inferences	• Places and activities in the community • Directions • People and things in a train station	• Present continuous statements and questions • *Wh-* questions
3 **Dollars and Cents** *page 36*	• Talk about expenses • Talk about purchases • Talk about money • Talk about banking services • Listen to an automated phone message **Pronunciation Focus:** *Ng* versus *Nk*	• Read and complete a check register • Read and interpret a pay stub	• Classify information • Apply knowledge to new situations	• Personal expenses • Money: coins and bills • Banking	• Simple past statements • *Yes/no* questions + past tense • *Wh-* questions + past tense **Spotlight:** Simple past statements; questions with the simple past

Civics Concepts	Math Skills	CASAS Life Skill Competencies	SCANS Competencies (Workplace)	EFF Content Standards	Literacy Completion Points (LCPs)
		• 0.1.1, 0.1.2, 0.1.4, 0.1.5, 0.1.6, 0.2.1, 0.2.4	• Sociability • See things in the mind's eye	• Communicate so that others understand	• 39.01, 39.03, 49.01
• Identify and give specific information about the president and vice president of the United States • Complete a driver's license application	• Practice different ways of saying numbers	• **1:** 0.1.2, 0.2.1, 7.4.4 • **2:** 0.1.2, 0.1.3, 0.1.6 • **3:** 0.1.2, 0.1.4, 0.2.4 • **4:** 0.1.2, 0.2.1, 0.2.4, 7.4.2 • **5:** 0.1.1, 0.1.2, 0.1.4, 0.2.1, 0.2.4 • **6:** 0.2.2, 1.9.2 • **7:** 0.1.2, 7.1.4, 7.4.7, 7.4.8 • **GS:** 0.1.2	Emphasized are the following: • See things in the mind's eye • Creative thinking • Reason • Sociability • Acquire and evaluate information • Organize and maintain information • Use technology to complete tasks	Emphasized are the following: • Communicate so that others understand • Reflect on and reevaluate your opinions and ideas • Use technology • Find and use community resources and services	• **1:** 39.01, 39.02, 43.05, 46.03, 49.01, 49.03, 50.02 • **2:** 39.02, 49.01, 49.03, 50.02, 50.04 • **3:** 39.04, 49.01, 49.03, 50.04 • **4:** 39.04, 49.01 • **5:** 39.01, 49.01, 51.02 • **6:** 39.01, 49.01, 49.11, 49.17 • **7:** 39.04, 49.01, 49.09, 49.17 • **GS:** 49.15, 50.02, 50.08
• Identify places and activities in the community • Give directions to places in the community • Identify addresses and telephone numbers of places in the community	• Measure time • Interpret schedules • Tell the time	• **1:** 0.1.2, 0.2.1 • **2:** 0.1.2, 1.1.3, 2.2.1, 2.2.5, 6.6.5, 7.4.8 • **3:** 0.1.2, 0.1.6, 2.2.1 • **4:** 1.1.3, 2.2.4, 2.2.5, 2.3.1, 6.1.5, 6.6.6, 7.2.3, 7.2.4, 7.4.4, 7.4.8 • **5:** 0.1.2, 0.1.6, 2.2.1, 2.3.1 • **6:** 0.1.2, 2.1.1, 2.1.2, 2.5.1, 2.5.3, 7.3.2 • **7:** 0.1.2, 2.2.5, 7.1.4, 7.4.7, 7.4.8 • **WS:** 0.2.3, 2.4.1	Emphasized are the following: • Use resources • Acquire and evaluate information • See things in the mind's eye • Use technology to complete tasks • Reason	Emphasized are the following: • Find and use community resources and services • Use technology	• **1:** 46.01, 49.01, 50.02, 50.05 • **2:** 43.02, 43.03, 49.01, 49.02, 49.09, 50.03 • **3:** 43.04, 49.01, 49.03 • **4:** 43.03, 49.01, 49.02, 49.09 • **5:** 43.04, 49.01, 51.03 • **6:** 40.04, 46.01, 49.01 • **7:** 43.03, 49.01, 49.09, 49.17 • **WS:** 49.11, 49.12
• Distinguish U.S. coins and bills	• Use coins and bills • Calculate change • Balance a check register • Compute deductions	• **1:** 0.1.2, 1.3.3, 1.5.1, 7.2.3 • **2:** 0.1.2, 0.1.6, 1.1.6, 1.2.4, 3.5.4, 3.5.5, 6.2.1 • **3:** 0.1.2, 1.8.2 • **4:** 1.8.1, 1.8.2, 6.2.5 • **5:** 0.1.2, 0.1.6, 2.1.7 • **6:** 1.8.2, 4.2.1, 6.4.3 • **7:** 0.1.2, 7.1.4, 7.4.7, 7.4.8 • **GS:** 0.1.2, 0.2.1	Emphasized are the following: • Acquire and evaluate information • Organize and maintain information • Analyze and communicate information • Use resources wisely	Emphasized are the following: • Manage time and resources • Provide for physical needs	• **1:** 42.04, 49.01 • **2:** 42.02, 49.01, 50.02 • **3:** 42.04, 49.01, 49.03 • **4:** 42.03, 42.04, 49.01, 50.03 • **5:** 42.02, 42.04, 49.01, 51.02 • **6:** 36.06, 49.01 • **7:** 42.04, 49.11, 49.17 • **GS:** 42.05, 49.08, 49.15, 50.02, 50.03, 50.08

CASAS and LCP standards: Numbers in bold indicate lesson numbers.   •   **GS:** Grammar Spotlight   •   **WS:** Writing Spotlight

v

Scope and Sequence

	Life Skills				
Unit	**Listening and Speaking**	**Reading and Writing**	**Critical Thinking**	**Vocabulary**	**Grammar**
4 **Plans and Goals** *page 52*	• Talk about goals • Talk about plans • Describe the workplace • Ask for and give advice • Listen to a recorded message **Pronunciation Focus:** Past tense endings	• Read and evaluate a website • Read a biography • Read and write a timeline • Read and interpret a school calendar • Take notes • Complete a registration form **Spotlight:** Important events	• Classify information • Sequence events	• Personal, educational, and work goals • People in the workplace	• Present conditional • Future with *be going to*
5 **Smart Shopping** *page 68*	• Exchange personal information • Talk about common purchases • Talk about shopping • Make exchanges, returns, and purchases **Pronunciation Focus:** Stress	• Read store flyers • Read an article about shopping • Write about shopping • Read a website for specific information • Read and write shopping tips	• Choose the best alternative • Compare	• Common purchases • Things and activities in a shopping mall	• Comparatives • Superlatives **Spotlight:** Comparative forms of adjectives; superlative forms of adjectives
6 **Food** *page 84*	• Talk about food • Ask for things in a restaurant • Order from a menu • Take food orders **Pronunciation Focus:** Intonation patterns in sentences and questions	• Read and interpret a bar graph • Read and write a menu • Read and write a recipe • Read a website for specific information • Read and interpret food labels **Spotlight:** Restaurant reviews	• Sequence events • Make inferences • Choose the best alternative	• Food • People and things in a restaurant • Food preparation • Food label ingredients	• *How much* and *How many* • Quantity words
7 **Relationships** *page 100*	• Talk about relationships • Talk about a wedding • Communicate in social situations • Talk about customs • Conduct an interview • Disagree politely • Offer help **Pronunciation Focus:** Suffixes and syllable stress	• Read and make a family tree • Read about a family • Read a website for specific information • Write interview questions	• Reason • Evaluate • Choose the best alternative	• Relationships • People and activities at a wedding • Types of communication • Family traditions	• *Whose* versus *Who's* • Two-word verbs • Nouns and adjectives **Spotlight:** Two-word verbs; count nouns and noncount nouns

Correlations to National Standards

Civics Concepts	Math Skills	CASAS Life Skill Competencies	SCANS Competencies (Workplace)	EFF Content Standards	Literacy Completion Points (LCPs)
• Interpret a school calendar	• Solve word problems	**1:** 0.1.2, 0.1.3, 0.2.1, 7.1.1, 7.1.4, 7.5.1 **2:** 0.1.2, 7.1.1, 7.1.2, 7.1.3, 7.1.4, 7.2.6, 7.4.4 **3:** 0.1.2, 4.4.1 **4:** 0.2.2, 5.1.4, 5.5.2, 6.0.3, 6.0.4, 6.1.3, 7.1.4, 7.4.8 **5:** 0.1.2, 0.1.3, 2.1.7 **6:** 0.2.2, 2.7.1, 7.2.3 **7:** 0.1.2, 7.1.4, 7.4.7, 7.4.8 **WS:** 7.1.4, 7.2.3, 7.4.8	Emphasized are the following: • See things in the mind's eye • Responsibility • Self-management • Organize and maintain information • Use technology to complete tasks	Emphasized are the following: • Use technology • Find and use community resources and services • Pursue personal self-improvement • Create vision of future for self and other family members	**1:** 37.02, 50.02 **2:** 35.03, 37.02, 49.01, 50.02 **3:** 35.01, 37.01, 49.01, 49.03, 49.11 **4:** 49.01, 49.08, 49.09, 49.16 **5:** 49.01, 51.04 **6:** 39.01, 42.01 **7:** 49.01, 49.09, 49.11, 49.17 **WS:** 49.08, 49.09, 49.11, 49.13, 50.05
• Explore a shopping mall • Understand shopping terms	• Calculate percentages • Calculate savings	**1:** 0.1.2, 1.3.9, 1.4.1 **2:** 0.1.2, 0.1.3, 1.2.2 **3:** 1.2.1, 1.2.1, 1.2.2, 1.2.3, 1.2.5, 6.2.2, 6.4.1, 6.4.3 **4:** 1.2.5, 1.3.7, 7.1.4, 7.4.2, 7.4.4 **5:** 0.1.2, 0.1.3, 1.2.2, 1.3.3 **6:** 1.2.4, 1.2.5, 1.3.1, 1.3.3, 1.3.5, 1.6.3, 1.7.1 **7:** 0.1.2, 7.1.4, 7.4.7, 7.4.8 **GS:** 0.2.1, 7.2.3	Emphasized are the following: • Decision making • Use resources wisely • Acquire and evaluate information • Organize and maintain information • Analyze and communicate information • Use technology to complete tasks	Emphasized are the following: • Manage resources • Find, interpret, and analyze diverse sources of information • Find and use community resources and services • Use technology	**1:** 45.01, 49.01, 50.04 **2:** 45.01, 49.01, 49.03 **3:** 45.01, 45.02, 49.01 **4:** 45.01, 49.01, 49.16, 50.04 **5:** 39.03, 39.04, 45.01, 49.01, 51.05 **6:** 45.01, 45.02, 45.05, 45.06, 49.17 **7:** 45.01, 49.01, 49.09, 49.11, 49.17 **GS:** 50.04
• Understand eating habits in the U.S. • Understand food labels	• Compute a tip • Compute the cost of a meal	**1:** 0.1.2, 1.1.3, 1.1.8, 1.3.8, 6.7.2, 6.7.5 **2:** 0.1.2, 0.1.3 **3:** 0.1.2, 0.1.3, 1.3.8, 2.6.4, 6.2.1, 6.4.3 **4:** 1.1.1, 7.2.2, 7.4.4 **5:** 0.1.2, 0.1.3, 2.6.4, 6.2.1 **6:** 1.3.8, 1.6.1, 3.5.1, 7.2.3 **7:** 0.1.2, 7.1.4, 7.4.7, 7.4.8 **WS:** 1.2.2, 2.6.1, 7.2.5	Emphasized are the following: • Decision making • Reason • See things in the mind's eye • Teach others new skills • Serve clients or customers • Use technology to complete tasks • Acquire and evaluate information	Emphasized are the following: • Pass on values, ethics, and cultural heritage • Educate self and others • Use technology	**1:** 49.01, 49.11, 49.17, 50.03, 50.07 **2:** 49.01, 49.03 **3:** 45.03, 49.01 **4:** 38.01, 49.14, 50.07 **5:** 45.03, 49.01, 51.05 **6:** 41.06, 49.08, 49.17 **7:** 49.01, 49.09, 49.11, 49.17 **WS:** 39.03, 45.01, 49.13
• Use postal services	• Calculate ounces and pounds	**1:** 0.1.2, 0.2.1 **2:** 0.1.1, 0.1.2, 2.7.3 **3:** 0.1.2, 0.1.4, 0.1.6, 2.7.3, 4.6.1 **4:** 0.1.2, 2.7.2 **5:** 0.1.2, 0.1.3, 0.1.4 **6:** 2.4.2, 6.1.3, 6.1.4, 6.2.3, 7.2.3, 7.3.2 **7:** 0.1.2, 7.1.4, 7.4.7, 7.4.8 **GS:** 0.1.2	Emphasized are the following: • Decision making • See things in the mind's eye • Work with people of diverse backgrounds • Organize and maintain information • Acquire and evaluate information • Use technology to complete tasks	Emphasized are the following: • Pass on values, ethics, and cultural heritage • Listen to and learn from others' experiences and ideas • Respect others and value diversity • Use technology	**1:** 39.02, 49.01, 49.09 **2:** 49.01, 49.03 **3:** 36.05, 39.03, 39.04, 49.01, 49.05 **4:** 49.01, 49.04, 49.06 **5:** 39.03, 39.04, 49.01, 51.05 **6:** 46.02, 49.17 **7:** 49.01, 49.09, 49.17 **GS:** 49.15, 50.01, 50.07

CASAS and LCP standards: Numbers in bold indicate lesson numbers. • **GS**: Grammar Spotlight • **WS**: Writing Spotlight

Scope and Sequence

		Life Skills			
Unit	**Listening and Speaking**	**Reading and Writing**	**Critical Thinking**	**Vocabulary**	**Grammar**
8 **Health** *page 116*	• Talk about parts of the body • Describe illnesses and injuries • Talk about experiences in an emergency room • Talk to health professionals **Pronunciation Focus:** *Can* versus *can't*	• Read a website for specific information • Write about an illness or injury • Read and interpret medicine labels • Read and write an accident report **Spotlight:** Personal stories	• Reason	• Parts of the body • Illnesses and injuries • Things and activities in an emergency room • Medicine labels	• *Should* and *shouldn't* • *Might* and *will*
9 **Home and Safety** *page 132*	• Talk about actions in the home • Talk about problems in the home • Talk about a fire emergency • Talk about weather forecasts **Pronunciation Focus:** *L* versus *R* sounds	• Complete a maintenance request form • Write an ending to a story • Write about an emergency • Read a website for specific information • Read about emergency procedures • Read fire safety tips	• Sequence events • Evaluate	• Household actions • Problems in the home • Fire emergencies • Weather	• Commands and requests • *Will* and *won't* **Spotlight:** Future with *will;* future conditional statements
10 **Work** *page 148*	• Talk about jobs and job skills • Talk about work experience • Ask for information in a library • Communicate with an employer **Pronunciation Focus:** Intonation in *Yes/No* and *Wh-* questions	• Read and write job tips • Read job ads • Read and interpret a job application **Spotlight:** Résumés	• Evaluate	• Occupations and skills • People and things in the workplace • Job ads	• *Have to/don't have to* • *Would like/would rather*

Correlations to National Standards

Civics Concepts	Math Skills	CASAS Life Skill Competencies	SCANS Competencies (Workplace)	EFF Content Standards	Literacy Completion Points (LCPs)
• Explore an emergency room • Report work accidents	• Calculate ounces, tablespoon, and teaspoons	• **1:** 0.1.2, 3.1.1, 3.5.9, 7.4.8 • **2:** 0.1.2, 2.5.3, 3.1.1, 7.3.2, 7.4.4 • **3:** 0.1.2, 3.1.1, 3.4.3 • **4:** 3.3.1, 3.3.2, 3.3.3, 3.4.1, 6.1.5, 6.3.5, 7.4.2 • **5:** 0.1.2, 3.1.1, 3.1.3 • **6:** 0.1.2, 0.1.6, 3.1.1, 4.3.4 • **7:** 0.1.2, 7.1.4, 7.4.7, 7.4.8 • **WS:** 0.1.2, 7.2.2	Emphasized are the following: • See things in the mind's eye • Use resources wisely • Use technology to complete tasks • Organize and maintain information • Acquire and evaluate information • Work within the system	Emphasized are the following: • Find and use community resources and services • Use technology • Communicate with others inside and outside the organization	• **1:** 41.01, 49.01, 49.09, 49.17 • **2:** 41.01, 46.01, 49.01, • **3:** 41.03, 49.01, 49.03 • **4:** 41.04, 49.01, 49.17 • **5:** 41.03, 49.01, 50.02 • **6:** 39.01, 41.03, 44.01, 49.01, 49.09, 49.11 • **7:** 41.03, 49.01, 49.17 • **WS:** 41.03, 49.08, 49.13
• Understand emergency procedures • Practice fire safety in the home	• Convert temperatures	• **1:** 0.1.2, 0.1.3 • **2:** 0.1.2, 0.1.3, 1.4.7, 7.2.3 • **3:** 1.4.7, 7.2.2, 7.3.1 • **4:** 1.1.5, 2.3.3, 6.1.5, 7.4.2, 7.4.4 • **5:** 0.1.2, 0.1.3, 2.3.3, 7.2.2 • **6:** 1.4.8, 7.3.1 • **7:** 0.1.2, 7.1.4, 7.4.7, 7.4.8 • **GS:** 0.1.2, 7.2.4	Emphasized are the following: • Reason • See things in the mind's eye • Use technology to complete tasks • Organize and maintain information	Emphasized are the following: • Provide for physical needs • Use technology	• **1:** 38.01, 49.01, 50.02 • **2:** 38.01, 45.07, 45.08, 49.01, 49.11 • **3:** 44.01, 44.02, 49.03, 49.08 • **4:** 38.01, 44.01, 47.01, 47.02, 49.13 • **5:** 47.01, 49.01, 51.02 • **6:** 44.01, 49.04 • **7:** 45.08, 49.01, 49.09, 49.11, 49.17 • **GS:** 49.01, 50.02
• Recognize appropriate work behavior • Understand how to look for and apply for a job	• Compute overtime pay	• **1:** 0.1.2, 4.1.8 • **2:** 0.1.2, 4.1.8, 4.1.9, 7.5.1 • **3:** 0.1.2, 4.1.6 • **4:** 2.5.6, 4.4.1, 6.2.5, 7.4.2 • **5:** 0.1.2, 4.1.5, 4.6.4 • **6:** 4.1.2, 4.1.3 • **7:** 0.1.2, 7.1.4, 7.4.7, 7.4.8 • **WS:** 0.2.2, 4.1.2	Emphasized are the following: • Integrity and honesty • Acquire and evaluate information • Organize and maintain information	Emphasized are the following: • Find and use community resources and services • Pursue personal self-improvement • Educate self and others • Take responsibility for work quality and results • Communicate with others inside and outside the organization	• **1:** 35.01, 35.02, 49.01, 50.02 • **2:** 35.01, 35.02, 35.03, 49.01, 50.02 • **3:** 35.03, 36.01, 49.01, 49.03 • **4:** 35.04, 36.03, 37.04, 46.01 • **5:** 36.02, 36.05, 49.01, 51.05 • **6:** 35.04, 49.17 • **7:** 49.01, 49.09, 49.17 • **WS:** 35.05, 49.11

CASAS and LCP standards: Numbers in bold indicate lesson numbers. • **GS:** Grammar Spotlight • **WS:** Writing Spotlight

ix

All-Star is a four-level, standards-based series for English learners featuring a picture-dictionary approach to vocabulary building. "Big picture" scenes in each unit provide springboards to a wealth of activities developing all of the language skills.

An accessible and predictable sequence of lessons in each unit systematically builds language and math skills around life-skill topics. *All-Star* presents family, work, *and* community topics in each unit, and provides alternate application lessons in its Workbooks, giving teachers the flexibility to customize the series for a variety of student needs and curricular objectives. *All-Star* is tightly correlated to all of the major national and state standards for adult instruction.

Features

★ **Accessible "big picture" scenes** present life-skills vocabulary and provide engaging contexts for all-skills language development.

★ **Predictable sequence of eight, two-page lessons** in each unit reduces prep time for teachers and helps students get comfortable with the pattern of each lesson type.

★ **Flexible structure** allows students to customize each unit to meet a variety of student needs and curricular objectives, with application lessons addressing family, work, and community topics in both the Student Book and Workbook.

★ **Comprehensive coverage of key standards, such as CASAS, SCANS, EFF, and LCPs,** prepares students to master a broad range of critical competencies.

★ **Multiple assessment measures** like CASAS-style tests and performance-based assessment offer a broad range of options for monitoring and assessing learner progress.

★ **Dynamic, Interactive CD-ROM program** integrates language, literacy, and numeracy skill building with computer practice.

The Complete *All-Star* Program

★ The **Student Book** features ten, 16-page units, integrating listening, speaking, reading, writing, grammar, math, and pronunciation skills with life-skill topics, critical thinking activities, and civics concepts. The themes in Student Book 2 are related on a unit-by-unit basis to those in Student Book 1, making it easy to use both texts in multi-level classrooms.

★ The **Student Book with Audio Highlights** provides students with audio recordings of all of the dialogs in the Student Book. This audio CD also includes recordings of all of the new vocabulary presented in the "big picture" scenes.

★ The **Teacher's Edition with Tests** provides:

• Step-by-step procedural notes for each Student Book activity
• More than 200 expansion activities for Student Book 2, many of which offer creative tasks tied to the "big picture" scenes in each unit

• Culture, Grammar, and Pronunciation Notes
• Two-page written test for each unit (*Note:* Listening passages for the tests are available on the Student Book Audiocassettes and Audio CDs.)
• Audio scripts for all audio program materials
• Answer keys for Student Book, Workbook, and Tests

★ The **Interactive CD-ROM** incorporates and extends the learning goals of the Student Book by integrating language, literacy, and numeracy skill building with multimedia practice on the computer. A flexible set of activities correlated to each unit builds vocabulary, listening, reading, writing, and test-taking skills.

★ The **Color Overhead Transparencies** encourage teachers to present new vocabulary and concepts in fun and meaningful ways. This component provides a full-color overhead transparency for each of the "big picture" scenes.

★ The **Workbook** includes supplementary practice activities correlated to the Student Book. As a bonus feature, the Workbook also includes alternate application lessons addressing the learner's role as worker, family member, and/or community member. These additional, optional lessons may be used in addition to, or as substitutes for, the application lessons found in Lesson 6 of each Student Book unit.

★ The **Audiocassettes** and **Audio CDs** contain recordings for all listening activities in the Student Book. Listening passages for each unit test are provided at the end of the audio section for that unit.

Overview of the *All-Star* Program

UNIT STRUCTURE

Consult the *Welcome to All-Star* guide on pages xiv–xix. This guide offers teachers and administrators a visual tour of one Student Book unit.

All-Star is designed to maximize accessibility and flexibility. Each unit contains the following sequence of eight, two-page lessons that develop vocabulary and build language, grammar, and math skills around life-skill topics:

★ Lesson 1: Vocabulary
★ Lesson 2: Vocabulary in Action
★ Lesson 3: Talk About It
★ Lesson 4: Reading and Writing
★ Lesson 5: Conversations
★ Lesson 6: Application
★ Lesson 7: Review and Assessment
★ Grammar or Writing Spotlight

Each lesson addresses a key adult standard, and these standards are indicated in the upper right-hand corner of each lesson in a yellow bar.

SPECIAL FEATURES OF EACH UNIT

★ *Window on Grammar.* Grammar is presented and practiced in each unit in blue boxes called *Windows on Grammar*. These short presentations offer students small, manageable chunks of grammar that correlate with a variety of national and state standards. *Window on Grammar* boxes provide for written and oral practice of new language structures and functions. Students and teacher will find additional, in-depth grammar practice in a series of two-page lessons called *Spotlight: Grammar* presented throughout the book. A comprehensive *Grammar Reference Guide* at the back of the book summarizes all of the structures and functions presented.

★ *Window on Math.* Learning basic math skills is critically important for success in school, on the job, and at home. As such, national and state standards for adult education mandate instruction in basic math skills. In each unit, a blue box called *Window on Math* is dedicated to helping students develop the functional numeracy skills they need for basic math work.

★ *Window on Pronunciation.* The culminating activity in Lesson 5 (*Conversations*) of each unit is featured in a blue box called *Window on Pronunciation*. This special feature has two major goals: (1) helping students hear and produce specific sounds, words, and minimal pairs of words so they become better listeners and speakers; and (2) addressing issues of stress, rhythm, and intonation so that the students' spoken English becomes more comprehensible.

★ *Spotlight: Grammar* and *Spotlight: Writing.* At the end of each unit, students and teachers will find either a *Grammar Spotlight* or a *Writing Spotlight*. These are optional, two-page lessons that offer a supplementary focus on grammar or writing skill development.

TWO-PAGE LESSON FORMAT

The lessons in *All-Star* are designed as two-page spreads. Lessons 5–7 and the Spotlights employ a standard textbook layout, but Lessons 1–4 follow an innovative format with a list of activities on the left-hand page of the spread and picture-dictionary visuals supporting these activities on the right-hand page. The list of activities, entitled *Things To Do*, allows students and teachers to take full advantage of the visuals in each lesson, inviting students to achieve a variety of learning goals with them.

"BIG PICTURE" SCENES

Each unit includes one "big picture" scene in either Lesson 2 or Lesson 3. This scene is the visual centerpiece of each unit, and serves as a springboard to a variety of activities provided in the Student Book, Teacher's Edition, Color Overhead Transparencies package, and Interactive CD-ROM program. In the Student Book, the "big picture" scene introduces key vocabulary and serves as a prompt for classroom discussion. The scenes feature characters with distinct personalities for students to enjoy, respond to, and talk about. There are also surprising elements for students to discover in each "big picture" scene.

The Teacher's Edition includes a variety of all-skills "Big Picture Expansion" activities that are tied to the Student Book scenes. For each unit, these expansion activities address listening, speaking, reading, writing, *and* grammar skill development, and allow teachers to customize their instruction to meet the language learning needs of each group of students.

In the Color Overhead Transparencies package, teachers will find transparencies of each "big picture" scene, which they can use to introduce the vocabulary and life-skill concepts in each unit. They can also use these transparencies to facilitate the "Big Picture Expansion" activities in the Teacher's Edition.

Finally, the Interactive CD-ROM program highlights an additional aspect of the "big picture" scenes in its listening activities. Students working with the CD-ROM program listen to a series of new conversations taking place between characters in the "big picture" scenes. They then work through a series of interactive activities based on these conversations and receive immediate feedback on their work.

CIVICS CONCEPTS

Many institutions focus direct attention on the importance of civics instruction for English language learners. Civics instruction encourages students to become active and informed community members. Throughout each *All-Star* unit, students and teachers will encounter *Try This* activities that introduce students to civics concepts and encourage community involvement. In addition, *Application* lessons provide activities that help students develop their roles as workers, parents, and citizens. Those lessons targeting the students' role as citizen encourage learners to become more active and informed members of their communities.

CASAS, SCANS, EFF, LCPs, AND OTHER STANDARDS

Teachers and administrators benchmark student progress against national and/or state standards for adult instruction. With this in mind, *All-Star* carefully integrates instructional elements from a wide range of standards including CASAS, SCANS, EFF, and the Literacy Completion Points (LCPs). Unit-by-unit correlations of these standards appear in the scope and sequence on pages iv–ix. Here is a brief overview of our approach to meeting the key national and state standards:

★ **CASAS.** Many U.S. states, including California, tie funding for adult education programs to student performance on the Comprehensive Adult Student Assessment System (CASAS). The CASAS (www.casas.org) competencies identify more than 300 essential skills that adults need in order to succeed in the classroom, workplace, and community. Examples of these skills include identifying or using appropriate non-verbal behavior in a variety of settings, responding appropriately to common personal information questions, and comparing price or quality to determine the best buys. *All-Star* comprehensively integrates all of the CASAS Life Skill Competencies throughout the four levels of the series. Level 2 addresses all of the CASAS Level B Life Skills test items on CASAS Test Forms 33, 34, 34X, 53, and 54.

★ **SCANS.** Developed by the United States Department of Labor, SCANS is an acronym for the Secretary's Commission on Achieving Necessary Skills (wdr.doleta.gov/SCANS/). SCANS competencies are workplace skills that help people compete more effectively in today's global economy. The following are examples of SCANS competencies: works well with others, acquires and evaluates information, and teaches others new skills. A variety of SCANS competencies is threaded throughout the activities in each unit of *All-Star*. The incorporation of these competencies recognizes both the intrinsic importance of teaching workplace skills and the fact that many adult students are already working members of their communities.

★ **EFF.** Equipped for the Future (EFF) is a set of standards for adult literacy and lifelong learning, developed by The National Institute for Literacy (www.nifl.gov). The organizing principle of EFF is that adults assume responsibilities in three major areas of life — as workers, as parents, and as citizens. These three areas of focus are called "role maps" in the EFF documentation. In the parent role map, for example, EFF highlights these and other responsibilities: participating in children's formal education and forming and maintaining supportive family relationships. Each *All-Star* unit addresses all three of the EFF role maps in its *Application* lessons. Lesson 6 in each Student Book unit includes one of the three application lessons for that unit. The remaining two application lessons are found in the corresponding Workbook unit.

★ **LCPs.** Florida and Texas document the advancement of learners in an adult program through their system of Literacy Completion Points (LCPs). *All-Star* Level 2 incorporates into its instruction the vast majority of standards at LCP Level C.

NUMBER OF HOURS OF INSTRUCTION

The *All-Star* program has been designed to accommodate the needs of adult classes with 70–180 hours of classroom instruction. Here are three recommended ways in which various components in the *All-Star* program can be combined to meet student and teacher needs.

★ **70–100 hours.** Teachers are encouraged to work through all of the Student Book materials, incorporating the *Grammar* and *Writing Spotlights* as time permits. The Color Overhead Transparencies can be used to introduce and/or review materials in each unit. Teachers should also look to the Teacher's Edition for teaching suggestions and testing materials as necessary.

Time per unit: 7–10 hours.

★ **100–140 hours.** In addition to working through all of the Student Book materials, teachers are encouraged to incorporate the Workbook and Interactive CD-ROM activities for supplementary practice.

Time per unit: 10–14 hours.

★ **140–180 hours.** Teachers and students working in an intensive instructional setting can take advantage of the wealth of expansion activities threaded through the Teacher's Edition to supplement the Student Book, Workbook, and Interactive CD-ROM materials.

Time per unit: 14–18 hours.

ASSESSMENT

The *All-Star* program offers teachers, students, and administrators the following wealth of resources for monitoring and assessing student progress and achievement:

★ **Standardized testing formats.** *All-Star* is correlated to the CASAS competencies and many other national and state standards for adult learning. Students have the opportunity to practice answering CASAS-style listening and reading questions in Lesson 7 of each unit (*What do you know?*), in Lesson 7 of the Workbook (*Practice Test*), and in the Interactive CD-ROM program. Students practice with the same item types and bubble-in answer sheets they encounter on CASAS and other standardized tests.

★ **Achievement tests.** The *All-Star* Teacher's Edition includes end-of-unit tests. These paper-and-pencil tests help students demonstrate how well they have learned the instructional content of the unit. Adult learners often show incremental increases in learning that are not always measured on the standardized tests. The achievement tests may demonstrate learning even in a short amount of instructional time. Twenty percent of each test includes questions that encourage students to apply more academic skills such as determining meaning from context, making inferences, and understanding main ideas. Practice with these question types will help prepare students who may want to enroll in academic classes.

★ **Performance-based assessment.** *All-Star* provides several ways to measure students' performance on productive tasks, including the *Writing Spotlights* and *Conversation Checks* that have corresponding rubrics in the Student Book to facilitate self-assessment. In addition, the Teacher's Edition suggests writing and speaking prompts that teachers can use for performance-based assessment. These prompts derive from the "big picture" scene in each unit and provide rich visual input as the basis for the speaking and writing tasks asked of the students.

★ **Portfolio assessment.** A portfolio is a collection of student work that can be used to show progress. Examples of work that the instructor or the student may submit in the portfolio include writing samples, speaking rubrics, audiotapes, videotapes, or projects. Every Student Book unit includes several *Try This* activities. These activities require critical thinking and small-group project work. As such, they can be included in a student's portfolio. The Teacher's Edition identifies activities that may be used as documentation for the secondary standards defined by the National Reporting System.

★ **Self-assessment.** Self-assessment is an important part of the overall assessment picture, as it promotes student involvement and commitment to the learning process. When encouraged to assess themselves, students take more control of their learning and are better able to connect the instructional content with their own goals. The Student Book includes *Learning Logs* at the end of each unit, which allow students to check off the vocabulary they have learned and skills they have acquired. The Workbook provides practice tests at the end of each unit. Students are invited to chart their progress on these tests on a bar graph on the inside back cover of the Workbook.

★ **Other linguistic and non-linguistic outcomes.** Traditional testing often does not account for the progress made by adult learners with limited educational experience or low literacy levels. Such learners tend to take longer to make smaller language gains, so the gains they make in other areas are often more significant. These gains may be in areas such as self-esteem, goal clarification, learning skills, and access to employment, community involvement, and further academic studies. The SCANS and EFF standards identify areas of student growth that are not necessarily language based. *All-Star* is correlated with both SCANS and EFF standards. Every unit in the student book contains a lesson that focuses on one of the EFF role maps (worker, family member, community member), and the Workbook provides alternate lessons that address the other two role maps. Like the Student Book, the Workbook includes activities that may provide documentation that can be added to a student portfolio.

About the author and series consultants

Linda Lee is lead author on the *All-Star* series. Linda has taught ESL/ELT in the United States, Iran, and China, and has authored or co-authored a variety of successful textbook series for English learners. As a classroom instructor, Linda's most satisfying teaching experiences have been with adult ESL students at Roxbury Community College in Boston, Massachusetts.

Kristin Sherman is a contributing author on *All-Star*, Student Book 2. Kristin has 10 years of teaching experience in both credit and non-credit ESL programs. She has taught general ESL, as well as classes focusing on workplace skills and family literacy. She has authored a number of workbooks and teacher's editions for English learners. Her favorite project was the creation of a reading and writing workbook with her ESL students at the Mecklenburg County Jail.

Stephen Sloan is Title One Coordinator at James Monroe High School in the Los Angeles Unified School District. Steve has more than 25 years of teaching and administrative experience with both high school and adult ESL learners. Steve is also the author of McGraw-Hill's *Rights and Responsibilities: Reading and Communication for Civics*.

Grace Tanaka is professor and coordinator of ESL at the Santa Ana College School of Continuing Education, in Santa Ana, California, which serves more than 20,000 students per year. She is also a textbook co-author and series consultant. Grace has 23 years of teaching experience in both credit and non-credit ESL programs.

Shirley Velasco is assistant principal at Palmetto Adult Education Center in Miami, Florida. She has been a classroom instructor and administrator for the past 24 years. At Palmetto, Shirley has created a large adult ESOL program based on a curriculum she developed to help teachers implement the Florida LCPs (Literacy Completion Points).

Welcome to All-Star

All-Star is a four-level series featuring a "big picture" approach to meeting adult standards that systematically builds language and math skills around life-skill topics.

Predictable unit structure includes the same logical sequence of eight two-page lessons in each unit.

Accessible, two-page lesson format follows an innovative layout with a list of activities labeled "Things To Do" on the left and picture-dictionary visuals on the right.

Comprehensive coverage of key standards such as CASAS, SCANS, EFF, and LCPs prepares students to master critical competencies.

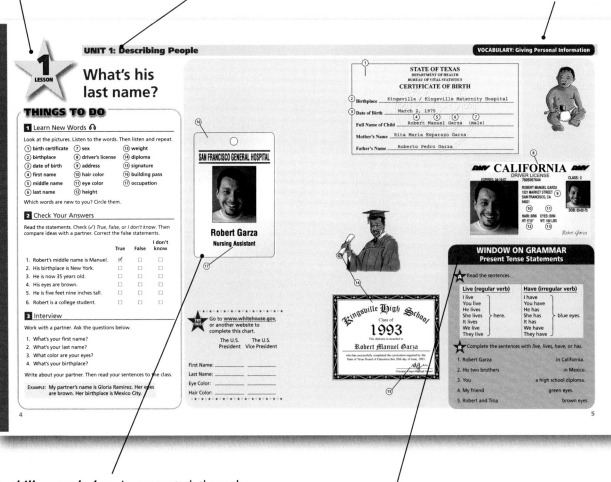

Life-skills vocabulary is presented through compelling realia and picture-dictionary illustrations. Students learn new words in a non-threatening, structured environment.

Windows on Grammar present manageable chunks of grammar with clear examples and follow-up activities. Grammar is addressed in greater detail in 5 lessons called *Spotlight: Grammar* throughout the book and in the Grammar Reference Guide at the back of the book.

"Big picture" scenes are springboards to a wealth of all-skills expansion activities in the Teacher's Edition and Interactive CD-ROM.

Color overhead transparencies for the "big picture" scenes provide fun and meaningful ways to present new vocabulary and concepts.

Structured speaking activities invite students to discuss the picture dictionary scene, simulate real-life conversations, and express their thoughts and opinions.

Reading activities develop critical thinking skills by asking students to find important information and make inferences.

Realia-based readings and narrative selections like maps, advertisements, descriptive paragraphs, poems, and short stories provide the basis for developing reading skills.

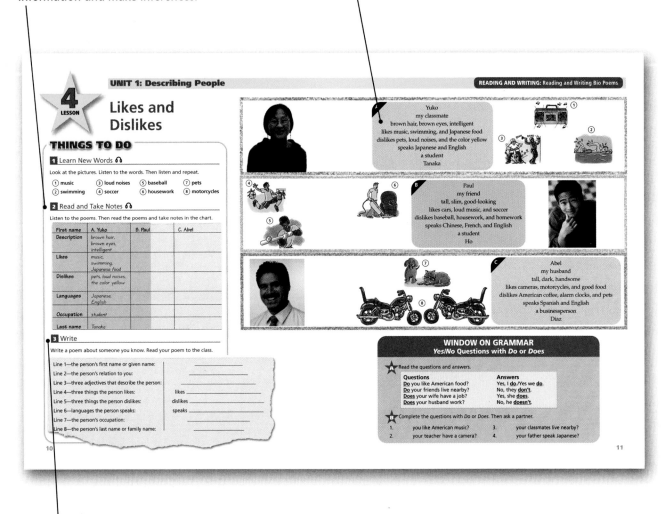

Abundant opportunities for writing prepare students for a variety of academic and real-world writing challenges, such as completing standard forms and writing complete sentences.

Try This **activities** promote civics concepts by connecting classroom learning to community experiences.

 Go to **www.whitehouse.gov**, or another website to complete this chart.

	The U.S. President	The U.S. Vice President
First Name:		
Last Name:		
Eye Color:		
Hair Color:		

Practice the Conversation activities invite students to engage in everyday conversations with their classmates, using the vocabulary and grammar they have learned.

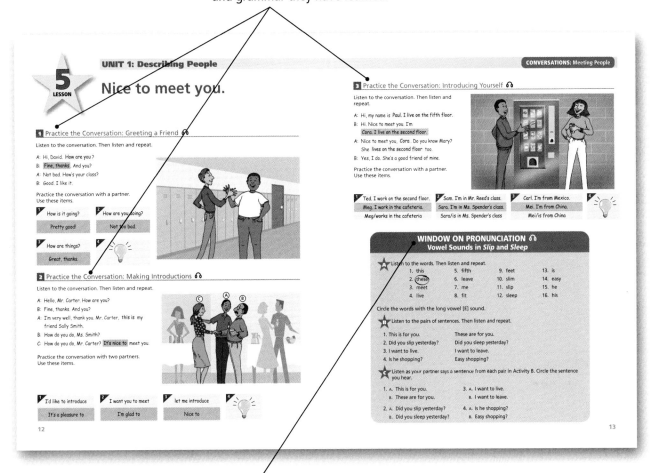

Windows on Pronunciation help students produce difficult sounds in English and address issues of stress, rhythm, and intonation.

Interactive CD-ROM program incorporates and extends the learning goals of each Student Book unit by integrating language, literacy, and numeracy skill building with computer practice.

Application lessons focus on developing the students' roles in life as workers, parents, and citizens.

Real-world documents and situations are highlighted in the *Application* lessons, exposing students to critical concepts they encounter at work, at home, and in the community.

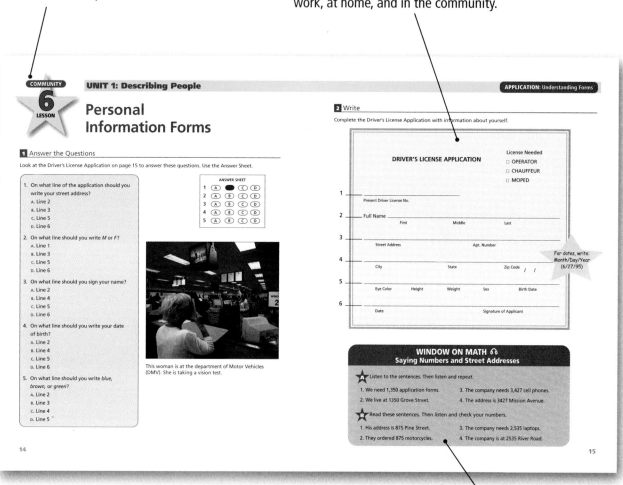

Windows on Math help students build numeracy skills for basic math work.

Alternate application lessons in the Workbook provide a flexible approach to addressing family, work, *and* community topics in each unit.

Listening Reviews help teachers assess listening comprehension, while giving students practice with the item types and answer sheets they encounter on standardized tests.

Conversation Checks are communicative information gap activities that also provide informal listening and speaking self-assessment tools.

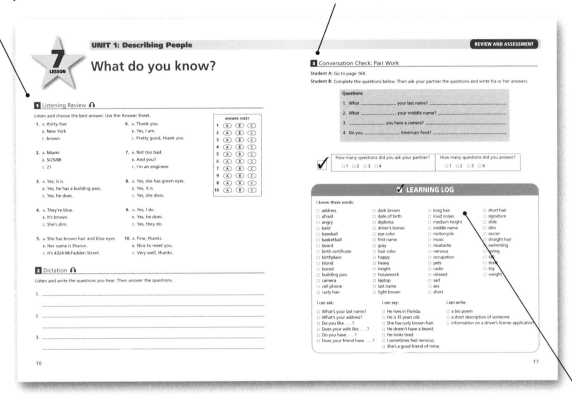

A *Spotlight: Grammar* or *Spotlight: Writing* lesson appears at the end of each unit, offering supplementary grammar or writing skill development.

Learning Logs ask students to catalog the vocabulary, grammar, and life skills they have learned, and determine which areas they need to review.

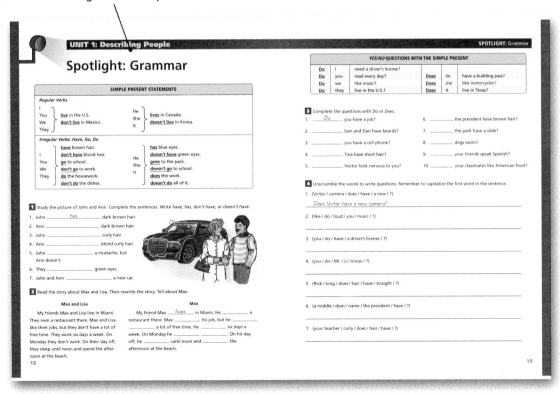

INTRODUCTION

Nice to meet you.

1 Practice the Conversation

Work with a partner. Practice the conversation.
Tell about yourself.

A: Hi. My name is _____.

B: Hi. I'm _____.

A: Nice to meet you.

B: Nice to meet you, too.

Introduce yourself to 5 more classmates.

2 Complete the Conversations 🎧

Use a question or sentence from the box to complete the conversations. Then listen and check your answers.

Useful Expressions

- Could you repeat that?
- How do you spell that? ✔
- What about you?

- What is _____?
- That's interesting!
- I'm sorry. I don't understand your question.

1. A: What's your name?

   B: Keiko.

   A: _____*How do you spell that*_____?

   B: K-e-i-k-o.

2. A: Where are you from?

   B: I'm from Mexico. _____?

   A: I'm from China.

3. A: What languages do you speak?

   B: Russian, French, and English.

   A: Really? _____!

4. A: Do you like to watch flicks?

   B: I'm not sure. _____ a flick?

   A: It's a movie.

   B: Then yes, I do.

5. A: Please turn to page 12.

   B: _____?

   A: Please turn to page 12.

6. A: Would you be interested in studying tomorrow?

   B: _____.

   A: Do you want to study with me tomorrow?

   B: Yes, thank you.

Work with a partner. Practice the conversations.

3 Follow Instructions 🎧

Look at the pictures. Listen to the classroom instructions. Then listen and repeat.

1 Listen to the words.	2 Say, "Hello."	3 Write your name.	4 Sign your name.
5 Check (✓) *True* or *False*.	6 Take out a piece of paper.	7 Practice the conversation.	8 Raise your hand.
9 Underline the word.	10 Circle the word.	11 Hand in your homework.	12 Listen and repeat.

Work with a partner. Take turns giving 5 instructions.

EXAMPLE:

A: Raise your hand.

B: Write your name and then circle it.

3

LESSON 1

What's his last name?

THINGS TO DO

1 Learn New Words 🎧

Look at the pictures. Listen to the words. Then listen and repeat.

①　birth certificate   ⑦　sex   ⑬　weight

②　birthplace   ⑧　driver's license   ⑭　diploma

③　date of birth   ⑨　address   ⑮　signature

④　first name   ⑩　hair color   ⑯　building pass

⑤　middle name   ⑪　eye color   ⑰　occupation

⑥　last name   ⑫　height

Which words are new to you? Circle them.

2 Check Your Answers

Read the statements. Check (✓) *True, False,* or *I don't know.* Then compare ideas with a partner. Correct the false statements.

	True	False	I don't know
1. Robert's middle name is Manuel.	✓	☐	☐
2. His birthplace is New York.	☐	☐	☐
3. He is now 35 years old.	☐	☐	☐
4. His eyes are brown.	☐	☐	☐
5. He is five feet nine inches tall.	☐	☐	☐
6. Robert is a college student.	☐	☐	☐

3 Interview

Work with a partner. Ask the questions below.

1. What's your first name?
2. What's your last name?
3. What color are your eyes?
4. What's your birthplace?

Write about your partner. Then read your sentences to the class.

> EXAMPLE: My partner's name is Gloria Ramirez. Her eyes are brown. Her birthplace is Mexico City.

⑯

SAN FRANCISCO GENERAL HOSPITAL

Robert Garza
Nursing Assistant

⑰

★ ★ ★ ★ ★ ★ ★ ★ ★ ★ ★ ★ ★ ★ ★ ★ ★ ★ ★ ★

TRY THIS Go to www.whitehouse.gov, or another website to complete this chart.

	The U.S. President	The U.S. Vice President
First Name:		
Last Name:		
Eye Color:		
Hair Color:		

★ ★ ★ ★ ★ ★ ★ ★ ★ ★ ★ ★ ★ ★ ★ ★ ★ ★ ★ ★

①

STATE OF TEXAS
DEPARTMENT OF HEALTH
BUREAU OF VITAL STATISTICS
CERTIFICATE OF BIRTH

② Birthplace _____ Kingsville / Kingsville Maternity Hospital _____

③ Date of Birth _____ March 2, 1975 _____

                  ④   **⑤**   **⑥**   **⑦**

Full Name of Child _____ Robert   Manuel   Garza   (male) _____

Mother's Name _____ Rita Maria Esparazo Garza _____

Father's Name _____ Roberto Pedro Garza _____

⑧

DMV CALIFORNIA DMV
DRIVER LICENSE
EXPIRES: 04-19-07   7805067644   CLASS: 2

ROBERT MANUEL GARZA
1521 MARKET STREET **⑨**
SAN FRANCISCO, CA
94821

⑩   **⑪**   DOB: 03-02-75

HAIR: BRN EYES: BRN
HT: 5'10"   WT: 160 LBS

⑫   **⑬**

Robert Garza

⑭

Kingsville High School
Class of
1993
This diploma ia awarded to

Robert Manuel Garza

who has successfully completed the curriculum required by the
State of Texas Board of Education this 20th day of June, 1993.

Principal, Kingsville High School

⑮

WINDOW ON GRAMMAR
Present Tense Statements

A Read the sentences.

Live (regular verb)	Have (irregular verb)
I live	I have
You live	You have
He lives	He has
She lives ⎱ here.	She has ⎱ blue eyes.
It lives	It has
We live	We have
They live	They have

B Complete the sentences with *live*, *lives*, *have*, or *has*.

1. Robert Garza _____ in California.

2. His two brothers _____ in Mexico.

3. You _____ a high school diploma.

4. My friend _____ green eyes.

5. Robert and Tina _____ brown eyes.

5

LESSON 2

She has curly brown hair.

THINGS TO DO

1 Learn New Words 🎧

Look at the picture. Listen to the words. Then listen and repeat.

1. long hair
2. short hair
3. straight hair
4. curly hair
5. bald
6. beard
7. mustache
8. tall
9. medium height
10. short
11. slim
12. heavy
13. blond
14. light brown
15. dark brown
16. gray

Which words are new to you? Circle them.

LINE STARTS HERE

2 Read and Write

Read these descriptions. Find each person in the picture. Write the correct name under each picture.

1. Robert is slim. He has short curly hair and a mustache.
2. Lisa has long blond hair and she's medium height.
3. Estela is short and slim.
4. Rick is short and heavy.
5. Dan is heavy and he has short straight hair.
6. Paul has dark brown hair and he is slim.
7. Sam has long straight hair and he is tall.

3 Practice the Conversation 🎧

Listen to the conversation. Then listen and repeat.

A: Would you give this book to Dan ?

B: I'm sorry. I don't know Dan .

A: He is tall and heavy . You can't miss him.

B: Tall and heavy ?

A: Right.

Practice the conversation with a partner. Ask about these people.

1 Robert	2 Rick	3 Sam	4 Paul
Robert	Rick	Sam	Paul
He has a mustache	He's bald	He has long hair	He is very tall and slim
A mustache	Bald	Long hair	Tall and slim

★ ★ ★ ★ ★ ★ ★ ★ ★ ★ ★ ★

TRY THIS Write a sentence about a classmate. Then read it to the class and ask, *Who is it?*

EXAMPLE: This person is <u>tall</u> and has <u>short</u>, straight <u>brown</u> hair and <u>brown</u> eyes. Who is it?

★ ★ ★ ★ ★ ★ ★ ★ ★ ★ ★ ★

Robert

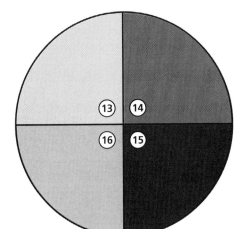

WINDOW ON GRAMMAR
Present Tense Negative Statements

A Read the sentences.

I **don't have** long hair.	We **don't have** beards.
You **don't have** blue eyes.	They **don't have** curly hair.
She **doesn't have** green eyes.	

B Complete the sentences with *have, has, don't have,* or *doesn't have.*

1. My teacher _____ blue eyes.

2. I _____ short curly hair.

3. The person next to me _____ a beard.

4. Paul _____ a mustache.

5. Don and Sam _____ blond hair.

7

3
LESSON

He looks tired.

THINGS TO DO

1 Talk About the Picture

Write 5 things about the people in the picture.

> EXAMPLES: Mei has long brown hair.
> Carlos is reading.

Share your ideas with the class.

2 Learn New Words

Look at the picture. Listen to the words. Then listen and repeat.

① happy   ⑤ afraid   ⑨ radio   ⑬ camera
② relaxed   ⑥ bored   ⑩ slide   ⑭ toy
③ sad   ⑦ angry   ⑪ swing   ⑮ laptop
④ nervous   ⑧ tired   ⑫ basketball   ⑯ cell phone

Which words are new to you? Circle them.

3 Practice the Conversation

Listen to the conversation. Then listen and repeat.

A: Lynn looks nervous .

B: She is. She is afraid of the dog .

A: That's too bad .

Practice the conversation with a partner. Use these ideas.

1 Amy/ happy	**2** Sue/ relaxed	**3** Alice/ sad	**4** Isabel/ angry	**5**
likes the slide	has a new book	misses her family	doesn't like the park	
great	nice	too bad	too bad	

★★★

TRY THIS Tell about yourself. Check (✓) *often, sometimes, hardly ever,* or *never.* Then compare your answers with a classmate's.

	often	sometimes	hardly ever	never	
I	☐	☐	☐	☐	feel happy.
I	☐	☐	☐	☐	feel nervous.
I	☐	☐	☐	☐	feel _____.

★★★

★4 LESSON

Likes and Dislikes

THINGS TO DO

1 Learn New Words 🎧

Look at the pictures. Listen to the words. Then listen and repeat.

1. music
2. swimming
3. loud noises
4. soccer
5. baseball
6. housework
7. pets
8. motorcycles

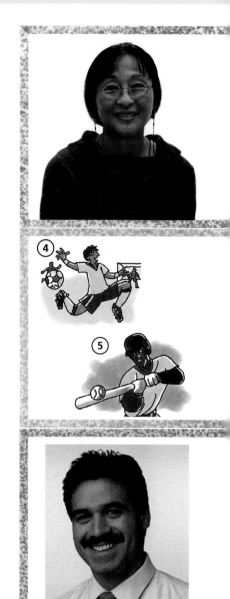

2 Read and Take Notes 🎧

Listen to the poems. Then read the poems and take notes in the chart.

First name	A. Yuko	B. Paul	C. Abel
Description	brown hair, brown eyes, intelligent		
Likes	music, swimming, Japanese food		
Dislikes	pets, loud noises, the color yellow		
Languages	Japanese, English		
Occupation	student		
Last name	Tanaka		

3 Write

Write a poem about someone you know. Read your poem to the class.

Line 1—the person's first name or given name: _____

Line 2—the person's relation to you: _____

Line 3—three adjectives that describe the person: _____

Line 4—three things the person likes: likes _____

Line 5—three things the person dislikes: dislikes _____

Line 6—languages the person speaks: speaks _____

Line 7—the person's occupation: _____

Line 8—the person's last name or family name: _____

A

Yuko
my classmate
brown hair, brown eyes, intelligent
likes music, swimming, and Japanese food
dislikes pets, loud noises, and the color yellow
speaks Japanese and English
a student
Tanaka

B

Paul
my friend
tall, slim, good-looking
likes cars, loud music, and soccer
dislikes baseball, housework, and homework
speaks Chinese, French, and English
a student
Ho

C

Abel
my husband
tall, dark, handsome
likes cameras, motorcycles, and good food
dislikes American coffee, alarm clocks, and pets
speaks Spanish and English
a businessperson
Diaz

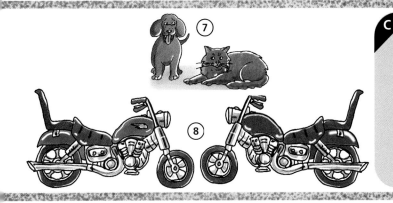

WINDOW ON GRAMMAR
Yes/No Questions with *Do* or *Does*

A Read the questions and answers.

Questions	Answers
Do you like American food?	Yes, I **do**./Yes we **do**.
Do your friends live nearby?	No, they **don't**.
Does your wife have a job?	Yes, she **does**.
Does your husband work?	No, he **doesn't**.

B Complete the questions with *Do* or *Does*. Then ask a partner.

1. _____ you like American music?

2. _____ your teacher have a camera?

3. _____ your classmates live nearby?

4. _____ your father speak Japanese?

11

LESSON 5

Nice to meet you.

1 Practice the Conversation: Greeting a Friend 🎧

Listen to the conversation. Then listen and repeat.

A: Hi, David. How are you ?

B: Fine, thanks . And you?

A: Not bad. How's your class?

B: Good. I like it.

Practice the conversation with a partner.
Use these items.

1 How is it going?
Pretty good!

2 How are you doing?
Not too bad.

3 How are things?
Great, thanks.

4 💡

2 Practice the Conversation: Making Introductions 🎧

Listen to the conversation. Then listen and repeat.

A: Hello, Mr. Carter. How are you?

B: Fine, thanks. And you?

A: I'm very well, thank you. Mr. Carter, this is my
friend Sally Smith.

B: How do you do, Ms. Smith?

C: How do you do, Mr. Carter? It's nice to meet you.

Practice the conversation with two partners.
Use these items.

1 I'd like to introduce
It's a pleasure to

2 I want you to meet
I'm glad to

3 let me introduce
Nice to

4 💡

3 Practice the Conversation: Introducing Yourself 🎧

Listen to the conversation. Then listen and repeat.

A: Hi, my name is Paul. I live on the fifth floor.

B: Hi. Nice to meet you. I'm Cora. I live on the second floor.

A: Nice to meet you, Cora. Do you know Mary? She lives on the second floor too.

B: Yes, I do. She's a good friend of mine.

Practice the conversation with a partner. Use these items.

1 Ted. I work on the second floor.
Meg. I work in the cafeteria.
Meg/works in the cafeteria

2 Sam. I'm in Mr. Reed's class.
Sara. I'm in Ms. Spender's class.
Sara/is in Ms. Spender's class

3 Carl. I'm from Mexico.
Mei. I'm from China.
Mei/is from China

WINDOW ON PRONUNCIATION 🎧
Vowel Sounds in *Slip* and *Sleep*

 Listen to the words. Then listen and repeat.

1. this	5. fifth	9. feet	13. is
2. (these)	6. leave	10. slim	14. easy
3. meet	7. me	11. slip	15. he
4. live	8. fit	12. sleep	16. his

Circle the words with the long vowel [E] sound.

 Listen to the pairs of sentences. Then listen and repeat.

1. This is for you.   These are for you.
2. Did you slip yesterday? Did you sleep yesterday?
3. I want to live.   I want to leave.
4. Is he shopping?   Easy shopping?

 Listen as your partner says a sentence from each pair in Activity B. Circle the sentence you hear.

1. A. This is for you.
   B. These are for you.

2. A. Did you slip yesterday?
   B. Did you sleep yesterday?

3. A. I want to live.
   B. I want to leave.

4. A. Is he shopping?
   B. Easy shopping?

Personal Information Forms

1 Answer the Questions

Look at the Driver's License Application on page 15 to answer these questions. Use the Answer Sheet.

1. On what line of the application should you write your street address?
   A. Line 2
   B. Line 3
   C. Line 5
   D. Line 6

2. On what line should you write *M* or *F*?
   A. Line 1
   B. Line 3
   C. Line 5
   D. Line 6

3. On what line should you sign your name?
   A. Line 2
   B. Line 4
   C. Line 5
   D. Line 6

4. On what line should you write your date of birth?
   A. Line 2
   B. Line 4
   C. Line 5
   D. Line 6

5. On what line should you write *blue, brown,* or *green*?
   A. Line 2
   B. Line 3
   C. Line 4
   D. Line 5

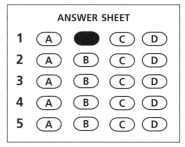

ANSWER SHEET

	A	B	C	D
1	(A)	●	(C)	(D)
2	(A)	(B)	(C)	(D)
3	(A)	(B)	(C)	(D)
4	(A)	(B)	(C)	(D)
5	(A)	(B)	(C)	(D)

This woman is at the department of Motor Vehicles (DMV). She is taking a vision test.

2 Write

Complete the Driver's License Application with information about yourself.

DRIVER'S LICENSE APPLICATION

License Needed

☐ OPERATOR

☐ CHAUFFEUR

☐ MOPED

1 _____
Present Driver License No.

2 _____ Full Name _____

First   Middle   Last

3 _____ _____

Street Address   Apt. Number

4 _____ _____

City   State   Zip Code   /   /

For dates, write: Month/Day/Year (6/27/95)

5 _____ _____

Eye Color   Height   Weight   Sex   Birth Date

6 _____ _____

Date   Signature of Applicant

WINDOW ON MATH 🎧
Saying Numbers and Street Addresses

 Listen to the sentences. Then listen and repeat.

1. We need 1,350 application forms.

2. We live at 1350 Grove Street.

3. The company needs 3,427 cell phones.

4. The address is 3427 Mission Avenue.

 Read these sentences. Then listen and check your numbers.

1. His address is 875 Pine Street.

2. They ordered 875 motorcycles.

3. The company needs 2,535 laptops.

4. The company is at 2535 River Road.

7
LESSON

What do you know?

1 Listening Review 🎧

Listen and choose the best answer. Use the Answer Sheet.

1. A. thirty-five
   B. New York
   C. brown

2. A. Miami
   B. 5/25/88
   C. 21

3. A. Yes, it is.
   B. Yes, he has a building pass.
   C. Yes, he does.

4. A. They're blue.
   B. It's brown.
   C. She's slim.

5. A. She has brown hair and blue eyes.
   B. Her name is Sharon.
   C. It's 4324 McFadden Street.

6. A. Thank you.
   B. Yes, I am.
   C. Pretty good, thank you.

7. A. Not too bad.
   B. And you?
   C. I'm an engineer.

8. A. Yes, she has green eyes.
   B. Yes, it is.
   C. Yes, she does.

9. A. Yes, I do.
   B. Yes, he does.
   C. Yes, they do.

10. A. Fine, thanks.
    B. Nice to meet you.
    C. Very well, thanks.

ANSWER SHEET

	A	B	C
1	Ⓐ	Ⓑ	Ⓒ
2	Ⓐ	Ⓑ	Ⓒ
3	Ⓐ	Ⓑ	Ⓒ
4	Ⓐ	Ⓑ	Ⓒ
5	Ⓐ	Ⓑ	Ⓒ
6	Ⓐ	Ⓑ	Ⓒ
7	Ⓐ	Ⓑ	Ⓒ
8	Ⓐ	Ⓑ	Ⓒ
9	Ⓐ	Ⓑ	Ⓒ
10	Ⓐ	Ⓑ	Ⓒ

2 Dictation 🎧

Listen and write the questions you hear. Then answer the questions.

1. _____

   _____

2. _____

   _____

3. _____

   _____

3 Conversation Check: Pair Work

Student A: Go to page 164.

Student B: Complete the questions below. Then ask your partner the questions and write his or her answers.

Questions

1. What _____ your last name? _____

2. What _____ your middle name? _____

3. _____ you have a camera? _____

4. Do you _____ American food? _____

✔

How many questions did you ask your partner?	How many questions did you answer?
☐ 1 ☐ 2 ☐ 3 ☐ 4	☐ 1 ☐ 2 ☐ 3 ☐ 4

✔ LEARNING LOG

I know these words:

- ☐ address
- ☐ afraid
- ☐ angry
- ☐ bald
- ☐ baseball
- ☐ basketball
- ☐ beard
- ☐ birth certificate
- ☐ birthplace
- ☐ blond
- ☐ bored
- ☐ building pass
- ☐ camera
- ☐ cell phone
- ☐ curly hair

- ☐ dark brown
- ☐ date of birth
- ☐ diploma
- ☐ driver's license
- ☐ eye color
- ☐ first name
- ☐ gray
- ☐ hair color
- ☐ happy
- ☐ heavy
- ☐ height
- ☐ housework
- ☐ laptop
- ☐ last name
- ☐ light brown

- ☐ long hair
- ☐ loud noises
- ☐ medium height
- ☐ middle name
- ☐ motorcycle
- ☐ music
- ☐ mustache
- ☐ nervous
- ☐ occupation
- ☐ pets
- ☐ radio
- ☐ relaxed
- ☐ sad
- ☐ sex
- ☐ short

- ☐ short hair
- ☐ signature
- ☐ slide
- ☐ slim
- ☐ soccer
- ☐ straight hair
- ☐ swimming
- ☐ swing
- ☐ tall
- ☐ tired
- ☐ toy
- ☐ weight

I can ask:

- ☐ What's your last name?
- ☐ What's your address?
- ☐ Do you like . . . ?
- ☐ Does your wife like . . . ?
- ☐ Do you have . . . ?
- ☐ Does your friend have . . . ?

I can say:

- ☐ He lives in Florida.
- ☐ He is 35 years old.
- ☐ She has curly brown hair.
- ☐ He doesn't have a beard.
- ☐ He looks tired.
- ☐ I sometimes feel nervous.
- ☐ She's a good friend of mine.

I can write:

- ☐ a bio poem
- ☐ a short description of someone
- ☐ information on a driver's license application

Spotlight: Grammar

SIMPLE PRESENT STATEMENTS

Regular Verbs

I
You
We
They
} **live** in the U.S.
don't live in Mexico.

He
She
It
} **lives** in Canada.
doesn't live in Korea.

Irregular Verbs: Have, Go, Do

I
You
We
They
} **have** brown hair.
don't have blond hair.
go to school.
don't go to work.
do the housework.
don't do the dishes.

He
She
It
} **has** blue eyes.
doesn't have green eyes.
goes to the park.
doesn't go to school.
does the work.
doesn't do all of it.

1 Study the picture of John and Ann. Complete the sentences. Write *have, has, don't have,* or *doesn't have.*

1. John _____*has*_____ brown hair.

2. Ann _____ brown hair.

3. John _____ curly hair.

4. Ann _____ blond curly hair.

5. John _____ a mustache, but Ann doesn't.

6. They _____ green eyes.

7. John and Ann _____ a new car.

2 Read the story about Max and Lisa. Then rewrite the story. Tell about Max.

Max and Lisa

My friends Max and Lisa live in Miami. They own a restaurant there. Max and Lisa like their jobs, but they don't have a lot of free time. They work six days a week. On Monday they don't work. On their day off, they sleep until noon and spend the afternoon at the beach.

Max

My friend Max ____*lives*____ in Miami. He _____ a restaurant there. Max _____ his job, but he _____ _____ a lot of free time. He _____ six days a week. On Monday he _____ _____. On his day off, he _____ until noon and _____ the afternoon at the beach.

YES/NO QUESTIONS WITH THE SIMPLE PRESENT							
Do	I	need a driver's license?				
Do	you	read every day?	**Does**	he	have a building pass?
Do	we	like music?	**Does**	she	like motorcycles?
Do	they	live in the U.S.?	**Does**	it	live in Texas?

3 Complete the questions with *Do* or *Does*.

1. _____*Do*_____ you have a job?

2. _____ Sam and Dan have beards?

3. _____ you have a cell phone?

4. _____ Tina have short hair?

5. _____ Hector look nervous to you?

6. _____ the president have brown hair?

7. _____ the park have a slide?

8. _____ dogs swim?

9. _____ your friends speak Spanish?

10. _____ your classmates like American food?

4 Unscramble the words to write questions. Remember to capitalize the first word in the sentence.

1. (Victor / camera / does / have / a new / ?)

   Does Victor have a new camera?

2. (like / do / loud / you / music / ?)

   _____

3. (you / do / have / a driver's license / ?)

   _____

4. (you / do / Mr. / Li / know / ?)

   _____

5. (Rick / long / does / hair / have / straight / ?)

   _____

6. (a middle / does / name / the president / have / ?)

   _____

7. (your teacher / curly / does / hair / have / ?)

   _____

1 LESSON

Where can you buy stamps?

THINGS TO DO

1 Learn New Words 🎧

Look at the pictures. Listen to the words. Then listen and repeat.

1. study
2. check out books
3. buy stamps
4. mail letters
5. mail packages
6. get cash
7. cash a check
8. fill a prescription
9. buy medicine
10. buy groceries
11. see a doctor
12. get a prescription
13. socialize
14. take classes
15. get something to drink
16. get something to eat

Which words are new to you? Circle them.

2 Ask Questions

Work with a partner. Ask about these things.

A: Where can you buy stamps ?

B: At the post office .

| 1 get cash | 2 buy medicine | 3 study | 4 💡 |

3 Interview

Work with a partner. Ask the questions below. Record your partner's answers.

EXAMPLE: A: How often do you buy stamps?
B: A few times a year.

How often do you ____?	every day	every week	every month	a few times a year
buy stamps	☐	☐	☐	☐
buy medicine	☐	☐	☐	☐
buy groceries	☐	☐	☐	☐
cash a check	☐	☐	☐	☐
see a doctor	☐	☐	☐	☐

Tell the class about your partner.

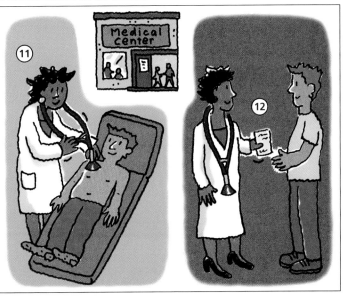

WINDOW ON GRAMMAR
Present Continuous

A Read the sentences.

I	**am**	**studying** at the library now.
You	**are**	**buying** groceries.
We	**are**	**shopping** at the supermarket.
They	**are**	**buying** stamps.
He	**is**	**eating** something.
She	**is**	**drinking** something.
It	**is**	**working** today.

B Complete the sentences with *am, are,* or *is.*

1. Jon _____ buying food at the supermarket.

2. I _____ doing my homework now.

3. Tom and Sam _____ working in a restaurant.

4. My friends _____ living in Florida now.

5. You _____ speaking English now.

UNIT 2: Going Places

How do I get there?

THINGS TO DO

1 Learn New Words 🎧

Listen to the words. Find the places on the map. Then listen and repeat.

① avenue   ⑥ across from   ⑪ go west
② boulevard   ⑦ block   ⑫ take a right
③ on the corner of   ⑧ go north   ⑬ take a left
④ between   ⑨ go east   ⑭ go straight
⑤ next to   ⑩ go south

Which words are new to you? Circle them.

2 Check *True* or *False*

Read the sentences. Look at the map. Check (✓) *True* or *False*. Then correct the false statements.

	True	False
1. The fire station is on Adams Boulevard.	✓	☐
2. The library is next to the drugstore.	☐	☐
3. The medical center is between Central and Green.	☐	☐
4. City Bank is north of the post office.	☐	☐
5. Central Avenue runs east and west.	☐	☐
6. Grove Boulevard runs north and south.	☐	☐

3 Practice the Conversation 🎧

Listen to the conversation. Then listen and repeat.

A: Excuse me. Where's the fire station ?
B: It's on Adams Boulevard between Diamond and Elm .
A: How do I get there from the Medical Center?
B: Just go north on Elm and take a left on Adams .

Practice the conversation with a partner. Ask about these places.

 1 community center   2 city bank   3 supermarket   4 restaurant

★ ★

Use the map to write directions. Read them to your classmates.

 TRY THIS

EXAMPLE: You are at the corner of Central and Diamond. Go north 4 blocks. Take a left on Grove. Go straight to the second street. What is on the corner?

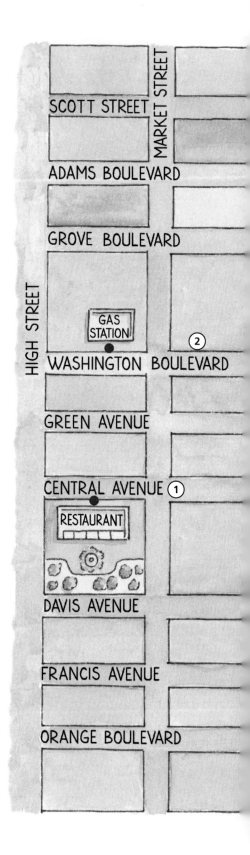

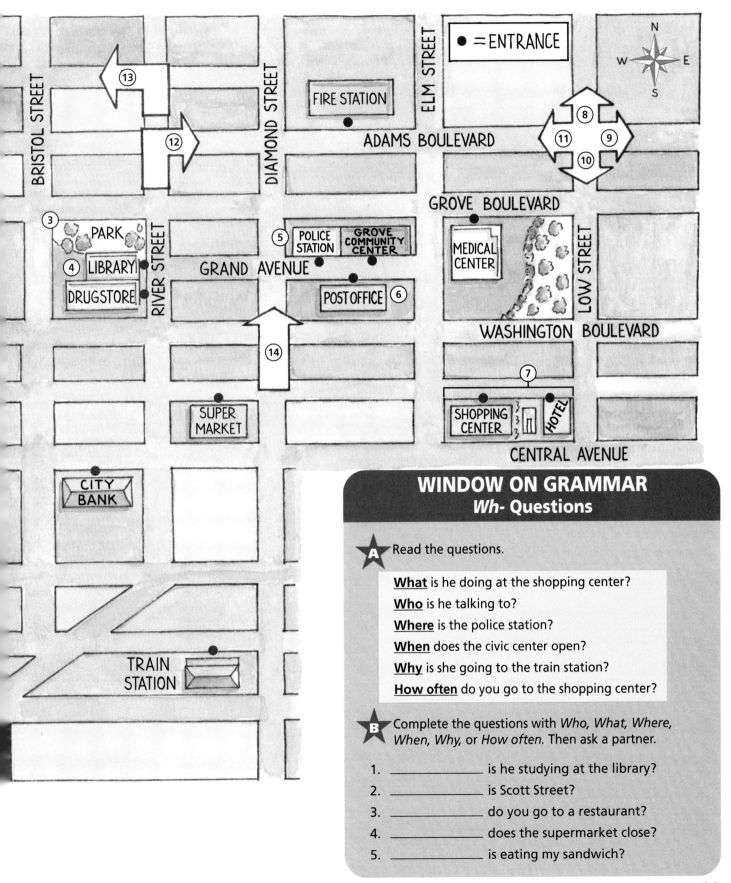

WINDOW ON GRAMMAR
Wh- Questions

A Read the questions.

What is he doing at the shopping center?

Who is he talking to?

Where is the police station?

When does the civic center open?

Why is she going to the train station?

How often do you go to the shopping center?

B Complete the questions with *Who, What, Where, When, Why,* or *How often*. Then ask a partner.

1. _____ is he studying at the library?
2. _____ is Scott Street?
3. _____ do you go to a restaurant?
4. _____ does the supermarket close?
5. _____ is eating my sandwich?

3 LESSON

It's next to the information desk.

THINGS TO DO

1 Learn New Words 🎧

Look at the picture. Listen to the words. Then listen and repeat.

1. ticket machine
2. ticket office
3. platform
4. track
5. snack bar
6. newsstand
7. information desk
8. waiting area
9. baggage check
10. pay phone
11. buy a ticket
12. wait for a train
13. read a train schedule
14. make a phone call
15. in front of
16. behind

Which words are new to you? Circle them.

2 Talk About the Picture

Write 5 things about the picture. Share your ideas with the class.

> EXAMPLES: Ruth is in front of the ticket machine.
> She is buying a ticket.

3 Practice the Conversation 🎧

Listen to the conversation. Then listen and repeat.

A: Excuse me. Where can I buy a ticket ?

B: At the ticket office .

A: Where's the ticket office ?

B: It's over there, next to the ticket machine .

Practice the conversation with a partner. Use the picture and the ideas below.

1 get a train schedule	2 buy a newspaper	3 make a telephone call
At the information desk	At the newsstand	At the pay phone
information desk	newsstand	pay phone
?	?	?

4 check my luggage	5 get something to eat	6
At the baggage check	At the snack bar	
baggage check	snack bar	
?	?	

LESSON 4

Train Maps and Schedules

THINGS TO DO

People on a commuter train

1 Check *True* or *False*

Study the map and read the statements below. Check (✓) *True* or *False*.

	True	False
1. Irvine is south of L.A.* (Union Station).	☐	☐
2. Covina is west of L.A. (Union Station).	☐	☐
3. The San Bernardino Line runs north and south.	☐	☐
4. El Monte is directly east of Baldwin Park.	☐	☐
5. Irvine is between Laguna Niguel and Oceanside.	☐	☐

Compare answers with your classmates and correct the false statements.
*Note: L.A. = Los Angeles

2 Read a Train Schedule

Read the train schedule and answer the questions below.

1. It's 7:00 in the morning and Carl is waiting at the Irvine station for a train to L.A. (Union Station). When is the next train?

    _____

2. It's 7:30 in the morning and Yun is sitting on train #683. Where is he now? _____

3. How long does it take to get from Irvine to Orange on train #601?

    _____

4. How long does it take to get from Oceanside to L.A. (Union Station) on train #603? _____

5. Which train is faster, #603 or #605? _____

3 Write

Write 2 true sentences and 2 false sentences about the map and schedule. Read your sentences to the class. Ask your classmates to identify and correct the false statements.

> EXAMPLES: The #683 leaves Oceanside at 5:56.
> L.A. County is north of San Diego County.

Counties in Southern California

★ ★

TRY THIS Use the Internet to get schedules for trains near you. Choose a place you want to visit. Print out a schedule of trains from your town or city to this place.

★ ★

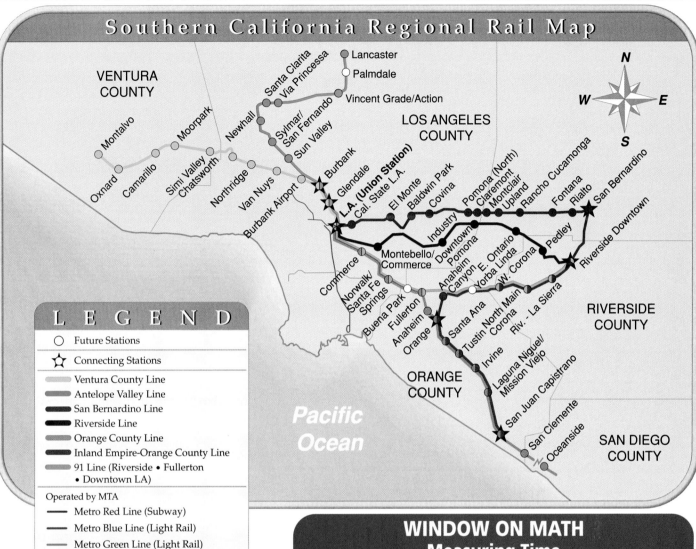

Southern California Regional Rail Map

LEGEND

○ Future Stations

☆ Connecting Stations

▬ Ventura County Line
▬ Antelope Valley Line
▬ San Bernardino Line
▬ Riverside Line
▬ Orange County Line
▬ Inland Empire-Orange County Line
▬ 91 Line (Riverside • Fullerton • Downtown LA)

Operated by MTA
— Metro Red Line (Subway)
— Metro Blue Line (Light Rail)
— Metro Green Line (Light Rail)

Southern California Regional Rail Authority

Train Schedule/Orange County

	601	603	605	683
Oceanside	4:47a	5:22a	5:56a	-
San Clemente	5:07a	5:43a	6:16a	-
San Juan Capistrano	5:16a	5:52a	6:25a	-
Laguna Niguel	5:23a	5:59a	6:30a	-
Irvine	5:33a	6:09a	6:40a	7:05a
Tustin	5:39a	6:15a	6:46a	7:12a
Santa Ana	5:46a	6:22a	6:53a	7:18a
Orange	5:51a	6:27a	6:57a	7:23a
Anaheim	5:55a	6:31a	7:01a	7:27a
Fullerton	6:02a	6:39a	7:09a	7:35a
Norwalk/S.F. Springs	L6:12a	L6:48a	L7:18a	L7:44a
Commerce	-	L6:58a	L7:28a	-
L.A. (Union Station)	6:40a	7:20a	7:50a	8:13a

L: Train may leave up to five minutes ahead of schedule.

WINDOW ON MATH
Measuring Time

60 seconds = 1 minute	60 minutes = 1 hour

A Complete the sentences.

1. 2 hours = _____ minutes

2. 5 minutes = _____ seconds

3. 120 seconds = _____ minutes

4. 275 minutes = _____ hours and _____ minutes

B Answer the questions.

1. It's 9:30. What time is it twenty minutes later? _____

2. It's 10:40. What time is it a half hour later? _____

3. The train usually leaves at 5:55, but today it is ten minutes late. When will it leave today? _____

27

When's the next train?

1 Talk About Time: Reading Clocks

Match the times with the clocks. Then practice saying the times.

a. 5:15

It's 9:30.

b. 6:10

c. 3:20

✓ d. 9:30

e. 1:10

f. 11:30

1. _d. 9:30_

2. _____

3. _____

4. _____

5. _____

6. _____

2 Practice the Conversation: Buying a Ticket 🎧

Listen to the conversation. Then listen and repeat.

A: I'd like a one-way ticket to Irvine , please.

B: Did you say one-way ?

A: Yes, that's right. When's the next train?

B: 5:15 .

A: 5:50 ?

B: No. 5:15 .

A: Okay. Thanks.

One Way
Chicago
↓
Los Angeles

Round-Trip
Chicago
Los Angeles

Practice the conversation with a partner.
Use these items.

1 a round-trip ticket to Chicago	2 a one-way ticket to San Diego	3 a round-trip ticket to Houston	4
round-trip/3:13	one-way/2:15	round-trip/4:40	
3:30	2:50	4:14	
3:13	2:15	4:40	

3 Practice the Conversation: Asking for Travel Information 🎧

Listen to the conversation. Then listen and repeat.

A: Is the 9 o'clock bus on time?

B: No, it's about fifteen minutes late.

A: Which platform will it be on?

B: Number 5 .

A: Thanks.

B: You're welcome.

Practice the conversation with a partner. Use these items.

Departure Schedule for Saturday, February 7

Departs	Arrives	Duration	Transfers	Platform
01:00a	03:45a	2h, 45m	0	9
03:00a	05:30a	2h, 30m	0	8
05:15a	08:55a	3h, 40m	0	3
06:00a	08:30a	2h, 30m	0	7
06:40a	09:50a	3h, 10m	0	6
07:00a	09:30a	2h, 30m	0	
08:00a	10:30a	2h, 30m	0	2
09:00a	11:59a	2h, 59m	0	5
09:30a	12:10p	2h, 40m	0	4
11:00a	01:30p	2h, 30m	0	
12:00p	02:10p	2h, 10m	0	1

h=hour m=minute

1 7:00
an hour / I don't know

2 12:00
20 minutes / Number 1

3 11 o'clock
30 minutes / I don't know

4 5:15
45 minutes / Number 3

5

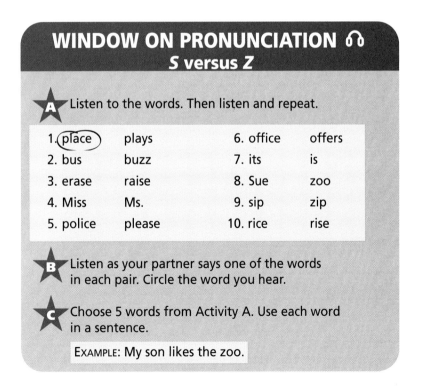

WINDOW ON PRONUNCIATION 🎧
S versus Z

A Listen to the words. Then listen and repeat.

1. place	plays	6. office	offers
2. bus	buzz	7. its	is
3. erase	raise	8. Sue	zoo
4. Miss	Ms.	9. sip	zip
5. police	please	10. rice	rise

B Listen as your partner says one of the words in each pair. Circle the word you hear.

C Choose 5 words from Activity A. Use each word in a sentence.

EXAMPLE: My son likes the zoo.

City Agencies

1 Answer the Questions

Read the questions below and look for the answers in the telephone directory on page 31.

1. You are new in town and you want to get a library card. What is the address of the library? _____

2. You want to know when the library closes today. What telephone number should you call? _____

3. You want to know which bus stops near the library. What number should you call? _____

4. You see a fire in a trash can in the park. What number should you call? _____

5. A dog bites you. What number should you call?

_____

6. People drive very fast on your street. You think it's dangerous. What number should you call? _____

TELEPHONE DIRECTORY
ALTON-CITY OF

AMBULANCE
Emergency Only... 911

FIRE DEPT. 17 City Plaza
To Report a Fire...911
Fire Chief...555-5940

LIBRARY 2258 N. Main St.
Hours.. 555-5849
Information Desk.................................555-3476

MEDICAL CENTER 140 Lincoln Ave.
General Information.............................555-9685

POLICE DEPT. 40 City Plaza
Emergency Only.. 911
Citizen Complaint Line.........................555-9685
Dog Officer...555-5746
Domestic Violence................................555-6958
General Business....................................555-6954

POST OFFICES
Washington Square...............................555-6845
459 S. Main St. 555-9445
1198 Cross Ave. 555-9347

PUBLIC WORKS DEPT. 594 S. Main St.
Parks and Recreation............................555-5584

SCHOOLS.. 555-4556

TRANSIT AUTHORITY
Bus Travel... 555-9887
Metrolink..555-4665

★ ★

TRY THIS Look in your telephone directory. Find the addresses and telephone numbers for these services in your town or city.

AMBULANCE _____

FIRE DEPT. _____

LIBRARY _____

POLICE EMERGENCY _____

POST OFFICE _____

★ ★

LESSON 7

What do you know?

1 Listening Review 🎧

Listen and choose the correct answer. Use the Answer Sheet.

1. A. Yes, I am.
   B. He is working at the supermarket.
   C. a few times a week

2. A. at the Civic Center
   B. at a gas station
   C. at a bank

3. A. at 9:15
   B. on Davis Avenue
   C. Yes, that's right.

4. A. He is using a computer.
   B. They are cashing their checks.
   C. They are studying.

5. A. It's next to the bank.
   B. Go north on Diamond and take your first right.
   C. You can get something to eat there.

6. A. track #2
   B. It's next to the snack bar.
   C. at the information desk

7. A. #604
   B. in fifteen minutes
   C. to L.A.

8. A. Yes, it is.
   B. No, they aren't.
   C. No, we aren't.

9. A. It's east of L.A.
   B. twenty minutes
   C. Yes, it does.

10. A. It's next to the post office.
    B. on Grand Avenue
    C. at the post office

ANSWER SHEET

	A	B	C
1	A	B	C
2	A	B	C
3	A	B	C
4	A	B	C
5	A	B	C
6	A	B	C
7	A	B	C
8	A	B	C
9	A	B	C
10	A	B	C

2 Conversation Check: Pair Work

Student A: Go to page 164.

Student B: Ask your partner questions to complete the map.

EXAMPLE: **B:** What's across from the bank?

A: the post office

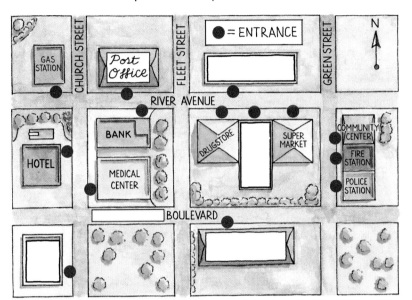

☑

How many questions did you ask your partner?
☐ 1   ☐ 2   ☐ 3   ☐ 4   ☐ 5   ☐ 6
How many questions did you answer?
☐ 1   ☐ 2   ☐ 3   ☐ 4   ☐ 5   ☐ 6

☑ LEARNING LOG

I know these words:

- ☐ across from
- ☐ avenue
- ☐ baggage check
- ☐ behind
- ☐ between
- ☐ block
- ☐ boulevard
- ☐ buy a ticket
- ☐ buy groceries
- ☐ buy medicine
- ☐ buy stamps
- ☐ cash a check

- ☐ check out books
- ☐ fill a prescription
- ☐ get a prescription
- ☐ get cash
- ☐ get something to drink
- ☐ get something to eat
- ☐ go east
- ☐ go north
- ☐ go south
- ☐ go straight
- ☐ go west
- ☐ in front of

- ☐ information desk
- ☐ mail letters
- ☐ mail packages
- ☐ make a phone call
- ☐ newsstand
- ☐ next to
- ☐ on the corner of
- ☐ one way
- ☐ pay phone
- ☐ platform
- ☐ read a train schedule
- ☐ round trip

- ☐ see a doctor
- ☐ snack bar
- ☐ socialize
- ☐ study
- ☐ take a left
- ☐ take a right
- ☐ take classes
- ☐ ticket machine
- ☐ ticket office
- ☐ track
- ☐ wait for a train
- ☐ waiting area

I can ask:

- ☐ Where can I buy a ticket?
- ☐ When does the civic center open?
- ☐ Why is she going to the train station?
- ☐ How do I get there?
- ☐ When's the next train?
- ☐ How long does it take to get to L.A.?
- ☐ Is the bus on time?

I can say:

- ☐ He is studying at the library now.
- ☐ Central Avenue runs east and west.
- ☐ The fire station is on Adams Boulevard.
- ☐ Go north on Main and take your first right.
- ☐ Take a left on Grove Street.
- ☐ I'd like a one-way ticket, please.

I can write:

- ☐ a description of a picture
- ☐ map directions
- ☐ schedule information
- ☐ an emergency telephone list

Spotlight: Writing

1 Read about the 5 main parts of a letter. Then label the parts of the thank-you letter below.

Main Parts of a Letter	Where	What
1. Heading	in the upper right corner	the writer's address and the date
2. Greeting	on the left side between the heading and the body	*Dear* + name + comma
3. Body	after the greeting	what you want to say in the letter
4. Closing	on the right side below the body	*Sincerely, Yours Truly,* etc. + comma
5. Signature	on the right side below the closing	the writer's name in handwriting

1034 Bristol Street
Austin, TX 78722

March 15, 2005 ---------- *Heading*

_____ ---- Dear Grace,

    Thank you so much for the beautiful
flowers. They are sitting on my table now as I
write this letter. I was very sick. Now I am
feeling much better thanks to all of the
attention from my friends.

        Sincerely, ----------

        Diedra ----------

2 Read about the 3 main parts of an envelope. Then label the parts of the envelope below.

Main Parts of an Envelope	Where	What
1. address	in the middle	the receiver's name and address
2. return address	in the upper left corner	the writer's name and address
3. stamp	in the upper right corner	the postage you buy to send the envelope

Diedra Smith
1034 Bristol Street
Austin, TX 78722

37¢

Grace André
526 Broadway Avenue
San Antonio, TX 78209

3 Write a short thank-you letter to a friend or relative. Include all 5 parts of a letter.

FOCUS ON WRITING: Using Commas

- Use a comma between the name of a city and state or state abbreviation.

  EXAMPLE: Austin, TX

- Use a comma between the day of the month and the year.

  EXAMPLE: March 15, 2005

- Use a comma after the greeting and closing in a letter.

  EXAMPLES: Dear Grace,
  Sincerely,

State	Abbreviation
California	CA
Florida	FL
Illinois	IL
New Jersey	NJ
New York	NY
Texas	TX

4 Address an envelope with your friend or relative's address. Add your return address.

37¢

LESSON 1

How much do you spend on groceries?

THINGS TO DO

1 Learn New Words 🎧

Look at the pictures. Listen to the words. Then listen and repeat.

Personal Expenses

(1) groceries   (8) utilities
(2) recreation   (9) gas
(3) toiletries   (10) electricity
(4) bus fare   (11) cash
(5) car repairs   (12) credit card
(6) car payments   (13) personal check
(7) rent   (14) money order

Which words are new to you? Circle them.

2 Interview

Work with a partner. Ask the questions below.

How much do you spend on ___?	$$$ a lot	$$ an average amount	$ not very much
groceries	☐	☐	☐
recreation	☐	☐	☐
toiletries	☐	☐	☐
bus fare	☐	☐	☐
rent	☐	☐	☐
_____	☐	☐	☐

Tell the class about your partner.

> EXAMPLE: My partner spends a lot on groceries, but he doesn't spend very much on recreation.

3 Find Someone Who

Talk to different classmates. Find someone who answers yes to your question. Write the person's name in the chart.

A: Do you use a credit card to buy groceries?

B: Yes, I do. / No, I don't.

Find someone who _____.	Person's Name
1. uses a credit card to buy groceries	_____
2. pays the electricity bill by money order	_____
3. pays the rent by check	_____
4. uses cash to buy groceries	_____

Transportation Expenses

(4)

(5)

Housing Expenses

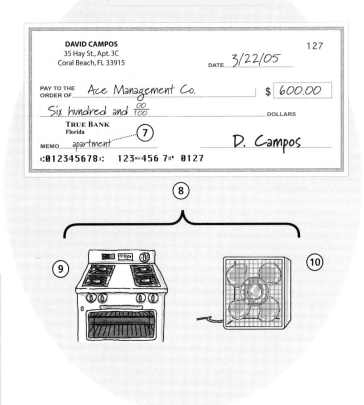

DAVID CAMPOS
35 Hay St., Apt. 3C
Coral Beach, FL 33915
DATE 3/22/05
127
PAY TO THE ORDER OF Ace Management Co. $ 600.00
Six hundred and 00/100 DOLLARS
TRUE BANK Florida
(7)
MEMO apartment   D. Campos
⑈012345678⑈ 123⑈456 7⑈ 0127

(8)

(9) (10)

DAVID CAMPOS
35 Hay St., Apt. 3C
Coral Beach, FL 33915
DATE 3/22/05
126
PAY TO THE ORDER OF cars-r-us $ 200.00
Two hundred and 00/100 DOLLARS
TRUE BANK Florida
(6)
MEMO car   D. Campos
⑈012345678⑈ 123⑈456 7⑈ 0126

Ways to Pay

(11)

(12)

(13)

(14)

WINDOW ON GRAMMAR
Simple Past Statements

A Read the sentences.

REGULAR VERBS

She **cashed** a check. | She **didn't cash** a money order.
He **needed** some toiletries. | He **didn't need** groceries.

IRREGULAR VERBS: BUY, GIVE, GO

We **bought** a new car. | We **didn't buy** a new house.
I **gave** him some cash. | I **didn't give** him a check.
I **went** to the drugstore. | I **didn't go** to the bank.

B Complete these sentences. Use the verbs in parentheses.

1. I _____ some food yesterday. (buy)
2. He _____ me a personal check. (not/give)
3. I _____ my paycheck last Friday. (cash)
4. We _____ to the bank to get some money. (go)
5. They _____ out yesterday. (not/go)

37

2 LESSON

Can you change a twenty?

The customer buys...

THINGS TO DO

1 Learn New Words

Look at the pictures. Listen to the words. Then listen and repeat.

① toothbrush   ⑥ penny (1¢)   ⑪ five dollars ($5.00)
② razor   ⑦ nickel (5¢)   ⑫ ten dollars ($10.00)
③ shaving cream   ⑧ dime (10¢)   ⑬ twenty dollars ($20.00)
④ shampoo   ⑨ quarter (25¢)   ⑭ fifty dollars ($50.00)
⑤ toothpaste   ⑩ dollar ($1.00)

2 Write

Complete the sentences with information from the pictures.

1. Dana bought a __toothbrush__ for $3.59. She gave the cashier ___$10.00___. He gave her _____ in change.

2. Sam went shopping at the drugstore. He bought a _____ and some _____. He gave the cashier _____. The cashier gave him _____ back.

3. Jim bought some _____ and some _____ for _____. He gave the cashier _____.

3 Practice the Conversation

Listen to the conversation in a store. Then listen and repeat.

A: The total is $1.25 .
B: Can you change a twenty ?
A: Sure. Your change is $17.75 .
B: Shouldn't that be $18.75 ?
A: Oh, sorry. You're right.

Practice the conversation with a partner. Ask about this money.

1 $5.15	**2** $10.50	**3** $41.14	**4**
a ten	a fifty	a fifty	
$4.75	$38.50	$8.56	
$4.85	$39.50	$8.86	

★ ★

 TRY THIS

Write 3 things you bought last month.

EXAMPLE: I bought shampoo for $4.29.

★ ★

The customer pays...

The customer's change is...

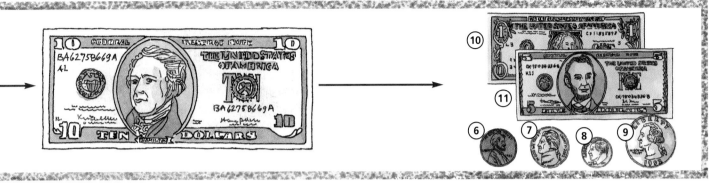

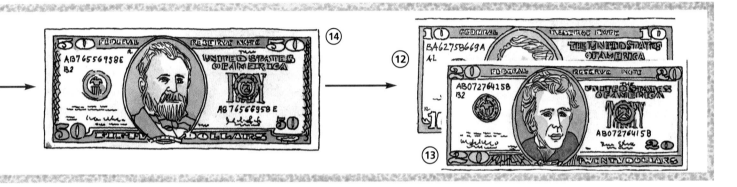

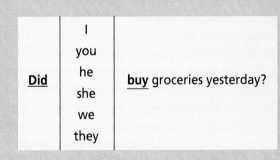

WINDOW ON GRAMMAR
Yes/No Questions + Past Tense

A Read the questions.

Did	I you he she we they	**buy** groceries yesterday?

B Ask a partner the questions.

	Yes, I did.	No, I didn't.
1. Did you use a credit card yesterday?	☐	☐
2. Did you spend any cash yesterday?	☐	☐
3. Did you make a car payment yesterday?	☐	☐
4. Did you write a check yesterday?	☐	☐
5. Did you cash a check yesterday?	☐	☐
6. Did you buy a money order yesterday?	☐	☐

I'd like to make a deposit.

THINGS TO DO

1 Learn New Words 🎧

Look at the pictures. Listen to the words. Then listen and repeat.

1. bank officer
2. bank teller
3. safe-deposit boxes
4. ATM
5. check register
6. checkbook
7. deposit slip
8. withdrawal slip
9. savings account
10. ATM card
11. monthly statement
12. paycheck
13. endorse a check
14. make a deposit
15. make a withdrawal
16. open a checking account

Which words are new to you? Circle them.

2 Talk About the Picture

Write 5 things about the picture. Then share ideas with the class.

> EXAMPLES: There are two bank tellers working now.
> The ATM is near the front door.

3 Practice the Conversation 🎧

Listen to the conversation. Then listen and repeat.

A: I'd like to make a deposit .

B: Do you have a deposit slip ?

A: Yes, I do.

B: Okay. I'll be right with you.

Practice the conversation with a partner. Talk about these things.

1	2
make a withdrawal	cash a check
a withdrawal slip	an account here

3	4
open a checking account	use the ATM
a photo ID	an ATM card

Marie

EMPLOYEES ONLY

TODAY'S RATES

Super Savings........1.2%

5 Year CD..............2.2%

10 Year CD............3.2%

Money Market........3.7%

WORLD SAVINGS

DEPOSIT BOXES

EXIT

ATM

Ali

Lea

Julia

PLEASE WAIT FOR NEXT AVAILABLE TELLER

Dan

Joe

Al

Dave

SEPT 17

LINE STARTS HERE

⑨ WORLD SAVINGS / WORLD BANK / PASSBOOK ACCOUNT

⑩ WORLD SAVINGS ATM CARD

⑪ WORLD SAVINGS STATEMENT

⑫ PAYROLL CHECK

⑬ Endorsements

⑭

⑮

⑯ WORLD SAVINGS New Checking Account Application

41

LESSON 4

Al's Checking Account

THINGS TO DO

1 Learn New Words 🎧

Look at the pictures. Listen to the words. Then listen and repeat

① **transaction amount**　② **balance**

2 Read and Take Notes 🎧

Read the personal checks and deposit slips and complete Al's check register on page 43. Then listen and check your work.

3 Answer the Questions

Answer the questions below. Then compare answers with the class.

1. How much money did Al have in his checking account on Sept. 26? _____ *$133.62* _____

2. How much money did he have on Sept. 30?
   _____

3. How many checks did he write in September?
   _____

4. How much money did he deposit in September?
   _____

BankTwo//
ATM

1234567890 1234567

AL MOORE
CKG ACCT 1234567890

BankTwo

DATE: 08-30-05
TIME: 15:22
ACCT: 1234567890

WITHDRAWAL: $60.00

THANK YOU
BANK/TWO

BankTwo

DATE: 09-26-05
TIME: 10:57
ACCT: 1234567890

WITHDRAWAL: $50.00

THANK YOU
BANK/TWO

★ ★

TRY THIS Complete Al's check #325. Use the information in the check register.

AL MOORE
8721 Vista Terrace
Miami, FL 33109

325

DATE _____

PAY TO THE
ORDER OF _____ $ [   ]

_____ DOLLARS

BankTwo
Florida

MEMO_____　_____ *Al Moore*

⑆012345678⑆ 123⑈456 7⑈ 0324

CHECK NO. or ATM	DATE	Check Register DESCRIPTION	① TRANSACTION AMOUNT	DEPOSIT AMOUNT	② BALANCE
ATM	8/30	Cash Withdrawal	$60.00		$385.89
325	9/4	Jon's Garage	$114.75		$271.14
326	9/16	Veritas Tel. Co.	$42.76		
ATM		deposit		$312.00	
	9/18	Bank Two			
ATM	9/26				
	9/30	deposit			

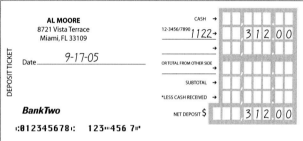

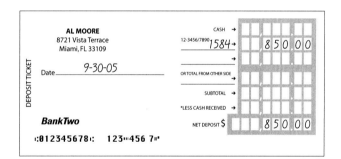

WINDOW ON GRAMMAR
Wh- Questions + Past Tense

A Read the questions. Then ask a partner.

> **Who did** you **talk** to yesterday?
>
> **What did** you **do** in the morning?
>
> **Where did** you **go** yesterday?
>
> **When did** you **get** up?
>
> **Why did** you **open** a checking account?
>
> **How much** money **did** you **spend**?

B Write 6 new questions. Ask a partner.

1. Who did . . . ?   3. What did . . . ?   5. Where did . . . ?

2. When did . . . ?   4. Why did . . . ?   6. How much . . . ?

43

LESSON 5

I'd like to buy a money order.

1 Listen and Write: Listening to an Automated System 🎧

Listen and write the missing words. Then listen and check your answers.

Thank you for calling Horizon Bank. For existing account information, press _____. For all other services, press _____. To speak to a customer service specialist at any time, press _____.

For checking accounts, press _____. For savings, press _____. For credit cards, press _____.

Please enter your checking account number followed by the # sign. For personal accounts, please enter the last four digits of your social security number followed by the # sign.

Your available _____ is _____.

2 Practice the Conversation: Buying a Money Order 🎧

Listen to the conversation. Then listen and repeat.

A: I'd like to buy a money order.

B: How much do you want it for?

A: Two hundred dollars .

B: Anything else?

A: No, that's all.

B: Okay. Your total is $205.00 .

Practice the conversation with a partner.
Use these amounts.

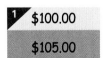
1 $100.00
   $105.00

2 $75.00
   $80.00

3 $90.00
   $95.00

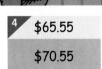
4 $65.55
   $70.55

5

3 Practice the Conversation: Asking for Change 🎧

Listen to the conversation. Then listen and repeat.

A: Do you have change for a twenty ?

B: I think so. How do you want it?

A: Do you have 2 tens ?

B: Sure. Here you are— ten, twenty .

A: Thanks.

Practice the conversation with a partner.
Use these items.

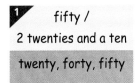
1 fifty /
2 twenties and a ten
twenty, forty, fifty

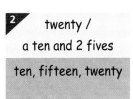
2 twenty /
a ten and 2 fives
ten, fifteen, twenty

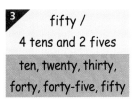
3 fifty /
4 tens and 2 fives
ten, twenty, thirty,
forty, forty-five, fifty

4

WINDOW ON PRONUNCIATION 🎧
Ng versus Nk

 A Listen to the words. Then listen and repeat.

bank	bang	saving	sink	think
thank	thing	sing	nothing	checking
ink	drink	long	wondering	young

 B Listen to each pair of questions below. Then listen and repeat.

Questions	Answers
1. What is that bank? What is that bang?	a. First National Bank. b. Something fell in the kitchen.
2. Do you have a sink? Do you have to sing?	a. Yes, in the bathroom. b. No, I can tell a story.
3. Now think. What do you want? Nothing. What do you want?	a. I can't. I'm too tired. b. I don't want anything either.

 C Now listen again. You will hear one question from each pair in Activity B. Circle the correct answer.

Pay Stubs

1 Learn New Words

Guess the meanings of the underlined words. Circle the best answer or definition.

1. Andy is an <u>employee</u> at Bank Two. He works as a bank teller. An employee is a _____.
   A. customer   B. worker   C. student

2. Andy's <u>salary</u> from Bank Two is $800.00 a week. His salary is his _____.
   A. rent   B. utilities   C. pay

3. Andy earns $800.00 a week, but Bank Two <u>deducts</u> $120.00 for taxes. He gets a paycheck for $680.00 every week. Another word for *deducts* is _____.
   A. adds   B. subtracts   C. equals

2 Answer the Questions

Read the pay stub. Answer the questions below.

BankTwo

Employee name: **Andy Kalish**

Period beginning: 02/01/05
Period ending: 02/15/05

SOCIAL SECURITY NUMBER: **928-62-5555**

FICA is a tax that is used to pay for retirement benefits, or Social Security.

Earnings	Hours Worked This Pay Period	Earnings This Pay Period	Earnings Year to Date
$20.00/hour	80	$1,600.00	$4,800.00
Federal taxes deducted		− $ 240.00	− $ 720.00
State taxes deducted		− $ 80.00	− $ 240.00
FICA		− $ 30.00	− $ 90.00
Health insurance		− $ 15.00	− $ 45.00
Check amount		$1,235.00	$3,705.00

1. What is Andy's pay per hour? *His pay is $20.00 per hour.*

2. How many hours did he work in this pay period? _____

3. How long is this pay period? _____

4. What was the amount of his paycheck this pay period? _____

5. How much was deducted from this check for health insurance? _____

46

3 Write

Complete the story and the deposit slip below. Use information from the pay stub in Activity 2.

Andy Kalish works ____40____ hours per week. He earns _____ an hour or $_____ a week. Every _____ weeks he gets a paycheck. In the last pay period, his earnings were $_____, but he got a paycheck for $_____. That's because the company _____ some money for taxes and health insurance. Andy deposited his $1,235.00 paycheck in his checking account. He took out $200.00 in cash. Complete his deposit slip.

DEPOSIT TICKET

ANDY KALISH
4832 Main Street
Houston, TX 77001

Date ___*2/17/05*___
(deposits may not be available for immediate withdrawal)

_____
(sign here if cash received from deposit) *

BankTwo

⑆012345678⑆   123⑈456 7⑈

CASH →

56-765/6789 →

→

OR TOTAL FROM OTHER SIDE →

SUBTOTAL →

*LESS CASH RECEIVED →

NET DEPOSIT $

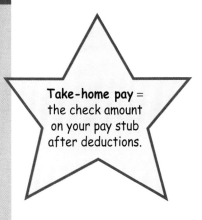

WINDOW ON MATH
Computing Deductions

 A Read the information below.

Employers deduct money for taxes and health insurance. The deduction for taxes depends on how much you earn and where you live. The deduction for health insurance depends on your insurance and your employer.

EXAMPLE: Sally Ying earns $10.00 an hour. Her employer deducts 20% for taxes and $25 from each pay check for health insurance. If she works 40 hours, she will get $295:
- $10.00 × 40 = $400
- $400 − 20% ($80) = $320
- $320 − $25 = $295

Take-home pay = the check amount on your pay stub after deductions.

 B Answer the word problems.

1. Jan earns $20.00 an hour. She pays 30% in taxes and $40 for insurance. How much does she take home in a 40-hour week?

2. Juan earns $15.00 an hour. He pays 25% in taxes and $35 for insurance. How much does he take home in a 40-hour week?

7
LESSON

What do you know?

1 Listening Review 🎧

Listen and choose the correct answer. Use the Answer Sheet.

1. A. I spent $500.00.
   B. very often
   C. not very much

2. A. by check
   B. a lot
   C. last week

3. A. Yes, I was.
   B. Yes, I do.
   C. Yes, I did.

4. A. Sure.
   B. Yes, I did.
   C. I have a credit card.

5. A. Do you have change for $10.00?
   B. Do you have a deposit slip?
   C. Do you have a withdrawal slip?

6. A. a safe-deposit box
   B. an ATM
   C. a teller

7. A. I filled out a withdrawal slip.
   B. It's about two hundred dollars.
   C. It's in my savings account.

8. A. twenty-five cents
   B. thirty-five cents
   C. forty-five cents

9. A. two hundred and twenty dollars
   B. fifty dollars
   C. thirty dollars

10. A. Yes. I have 2 tens.
    B. Yes. I have 2 fives.
    C. Yes. I have 5 ones.

	ANSWER SHEET		
1	A	B	C
2	A	B	C
3	A	B	C
4	A	B	C
5	A	B	C
6	A	B	C
7	A	B	C
8	A	B	C
9	A	B	C
10	A	B	C

2 Dictation 🎧

Listen and write the sentences you hear.

1. _____

   _____

2. _____

   _____

3. _____

   _____

3 Conversation Check: Pair Work

Student A: Go to page 165.

Student B: Ask your partner questions to complete this chart.

EXAMPLE: **B:** How much did Al spend on Monday?
A: Fifty dollars.

	Monday	Tuesday	Wednesday	Thursday
How much did Al spend?	*$50.00*	$2.00		
What did he spend it on?				
How did he pay for it?				

✔

How many questions did you ask your partner?	How many questions did you answer?
□ 1 □ 2 □ 3 □ 4 □ 5 □ 6	□ 1 □ 2 □ 3 □ 4 □ 5 □ 6

✔ LEARNING LOG

I know these words:

- □ ATM
- □ ATM card
- □ balance
- □ bank officer
- □ bank teller
- □ bus fare
- □ car payments
- □ car repairs
- □ cash
- □ check register
- □ checkbook
- □ credit card
- □ deduct

- □ deposit slip
- □ dime (10¢)
- □ dollar ($1.00)
- □ electricity
- □ employee
- □ endorse a check
- □ fifty dollars ($50.00)
- □ five dollars ($5.00)
- □ gas
- □ groceries
- □ make a deposit
- □ make a withdrawal
- □ money order

- □ monthly statement
- □ nickel (5¢)
- □ open a checking account
- □ paycheck
- □ penny (1¢)
- □ personal check
- □ quarter (25¢)
- □ razor
- □ recreation
- □ rent
- □ safe-deposit box
- □ salary
- □ savings account

- □ shampoo
- □ shaving cream
- □ ten dollars ($10.00)
- □ toiletries
- □ toothbrush
- □ toothpaste
- □ transaction amount
- □ twenty dollars ($20.00)
- □ utilities
- □ withdrawal slip

I can ask:

- □ How much do you spend on groceries?
- □ Can you change a twenty?
- □ Shouldn't that be . . . ?

I can say:

- □ I'd like to make a deposit.
- □ I spend a lot on car repairs.
- □ He earns $10.00 an hour.

I can write:

- □ information in a check register
- □ information on a deposit slip

49

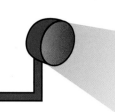

Spotlight: Grammar

SIMPLE PAST STATEMENTS		
Regular Verbs	*Irregular Verbs*	

I
You
He
She
It
We
They
cashed my paycheck.
didn't cash a personal check.

I
You
He
She
It
We
They
went to the park.
didn't go to the bank.

More Irregular Verbs			
present	**past**	**present**	**past**
buy	bought	leave	left
come	came	make	made
eat	ate	pay	paid
do	did	put	put
get	got	read	read
give	gave	see	saw
go	went	spend	spent
have	had	write	wrote

1 Complete each sentence below. Use the past tense.

1. I usually cash my paycheck on Friday, but last week I ___*cashed*___ it on Saturday.

2. We usually go to Miami, but last month we _____ to Sarasota instead.

3. She usually gives her son a dollar for lunch, but yesterday she _____ him five dollars.

4. Jan usually goes to work at 8. Yesterday, however, she _____ to work at 9.

5. This year they have a gas stove. Last year they _____ an electric stove.

2 Rewrite the following story. Use the past tense.

John wants to withdraw money from his checking account. He uses the ATM at the grocery store. First, he puts his ATM card into the machine. Then he types in his PIN (personal identification number). The machine asks him how much money he wants. John types in $100.00. Five twenty-dollar bills come out of the machine. The machine asks John if he wants a receipt. John presses the button for "yes". John checks the receipt to make sure it's correct. Then he puts it in his wallet with his $100.00.

___*John wanted to withdraw money from his checking account.*___

_____

_____

_____

_____

_____

_____

QUESTIONS WITH THE SIMPLE PAST					
Yes/No Questions			**Wh- Questions**		
	I		Who	**did**	I see yesterday?
	you		What	**did**	you do?
	he		Where	**did**	he cash his check?
Did	she	**go** to the bank yesterday?	When	**did**	she leave work?
	we		Why	**did**	it break?
	they		How much	**did**	we spend?
			How far	**did**	they go?

3 Unscramble the words to create questions. Then answer the questions. Remember to capitalize the beginnings of sentences.

1. (you / go / did / last Saturday / to work / ?)

   Question: _Did you go to work last Saturday?_____

   Answer: _____

2. (this morning / you / did / what / eat / ?)

   Question: _____

   Answer: _____

3. (money / you / spend / yesterday / how much / did / ?)

   Question: _____

   Answer: _____

4. (what / last week / buy / did / you / ?)

   Question: _____

   Answer: _____

5. (get up / did / when / you / this morning / ?)

   Question: _____

   Answer: _____

4 Complete the questions with *Who, What, Where, When, Why,* or *How much.* (More than one question is possible.) Then answer the questions.

1. _____ did you spend on bus fare last month? _____

2. _____ did she go after class last night? _____

3. _____ did they go to the movies with? _____

4. _____ did you do in class last week? _____

5. _____ did you go to New York? _____

LESSON 1

What are your goals?

THINGS TO DO

1 Learn New Words 🎧

Look at the pictures. Listen to the words. Then listen and repeat.

1. become a U.S. citizen
2. get married
3. buy a house
4. be a good parent
5. be a good citizen
6. get good grades
7. get vocational training
8. graduate from a university
9. get a GED
10. learn something new
11. get a job
12. get a raise
13. get a promotion
14. start a business

Which phrases are new to you? Circle them.

2 Write

List your goals in a chart like this. Then tell a partner about 3 of your goals.

Personal Goals	1. be a good parent 2.
Educational Goals	1. 2.
Work Goals	1. 2.

3 Find Someone Who

Talk to different classmates. Find someone who answers yes to your question. Write the person's name.

Find someone who wants to _____.	Person's Name
1. buy a house	_____
2. become a U.S. citizen	_____
3. get a job	_____
4. get a GED	_____
5. learn something new	_____

Personal Goals

1
2
3
4
5

Educational Goals

REPORT CARD
SOUTH BEACH CITY ADULT SCHOOL

Student Name: Brian Teese
Student ID: 7470   Year: 2004-05

Course	Number	Teacher	Grade
English	112	Mearek, S	98
World Civics	211	Colman, D	92
Earth Science	311	Bennet, H	93
Geometry	421	Tambrey, J	95

Absences: 0
Tardy: 0

Work Goals

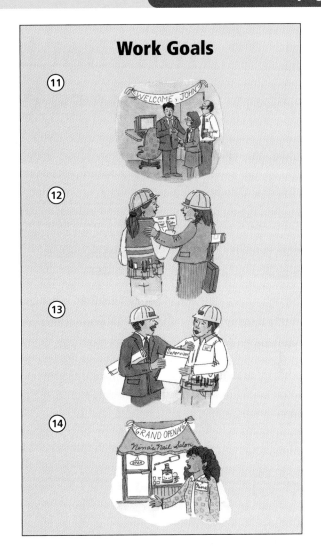

WINDOW ON GRAMMAR
Present Conditional with *Should*

A Read the sentences.

If you want to get good grades, you **should** study hard.
If he wants to buy a house, he **should** get a job.

B Complete the sentences. Use phrases from page 52 and your own ideas.

1. If you want to get a raise, you should _____
   _____ .

2. If you want to graduate, you should _____
   _____ .

3. If you want to start a business, you should
   _____ .

2 LESSON

You should take a business course.

(1)
SCHOOL

(2)

THINGS TO DO

1 Learn New Words 🎧

Look at the pictures. Listen to the words. Then listen and repeat.

① go back to school
② take a business course
③ save money
④ learn to use a computer
⑤ take a writing course

⑥ learn more English
⑦ vote
⑧ do volunteer work
⑨ read to your children
⑩ spend time with your children

Which words or phrases are new to you? Circle them.

2 Practice the Conversation 🎧

Listen to the conversation. Then listen and repeat.

A: Why are you saving your money ?

B: Because I want to start my own business .

A: That's great. Good luck!

Practice the conversation with a partner. Use these ideas.

¹ studying English	² going back to school	³ learning to use a computer	⁴ reading to your children
get a good job	get a promotion	get a raise	be a good parent

3 Write

Choose a goal. List 3 or more things you should do to reach the goal. Write your ideas in a cluster diagram like this one.

meet new people — take a class

Goal: to be a good parent

(9)
(10)

TRY THIS
Use the Internet to look for information about voting. Type in the phrase "voting in the U.S." Choose one site and evaluate it.

• This site (gives / doesn't give) useful information.

• The information at this site is (easy / difficult) to read.

Goal: to open my own clothing store

Goal: to be a good citizen

WINDOW ON GRAMMAR
Future with *be going to*

A Read the sentences.

I	**am going to go** back to school next year.	
He She	**is going to start** a business someday.	
You We They	**are going to take** a writing course.	

B Complete the sentences. Use the verbs in parentheses.

1. He _____ a doctor next year. (become)

2. I _____ a lot of money next year. (save)

3. My friends _____ in June. (get married)

4. I _____ next year.

55

LESSON 3

Who is going to get the job?

THINGS TO DO

1 Learn New Words 🎧

Look at the picture. Listen to the words. Then listen and repeat.

1. office manager
2. office worker
3. designer
4. bookkeeper
5. salesperson
6. supervisor
7. mechanic
8. late
9. on time
10. organized
11. disorganized
12. good with people
13. hardworking
14. lazy
15. bad attitude
16. good attitude

Which words are new to you? Circle them.

2 Talk About the Picture

Write 5 sentences about the picture. Then share ideas with the class.

> EXAMPLE: I think the office manager is angry.

3 Practice the Conversation 🎧

Listen to the conversation. Then listen and repeat.

A: Who's going to get the job as the new bookkeeper ?

B: I think Jon will. He's organized .

A: Yes, and he is always on time .

1 sales manager	2 supervisor	3 salesperson
Ben/hardworking	Tim/never late	Ken/ good with people
has a good attitude	is good with people	is always organized

4 Find Someone Who

Talk to your classmates. Find someone who answers yes to your question. Write the person's name in the chart.

Find someone who _____.	Person's Name
1. wants to supervise others	_____
2. is very organized	_____
3. is usually on time	_____
4. wants to work in an office	_____

Julie

Anton

Susan

Thomas

SERVICE

16 MANAGER SPECIAL

15

Mike

Laura

New

4 LESSON

A Success Story

THINGS TO DO

1 Preview

Look at the picture and read the title. What do you think the story is about? Check (✓) one or more ideas.

- ☐ a U.S. senator
- ☐ a doctor
- ☐ an important place
- ☐ an important person

2 Read and Underline

Read the story and underline the important events and years. Then answer the questions below.

1. When was Ben Nighthorse Campbell born? _____

2. How long was he in the Air Force? _____

3. When did he go to college? _____

4. When did he get married? _____

5. When did he become a U.S. senator? _____

Add the missing information to the timeline of Ben Nighthorse Campbell's life.

3 Write

List 5 important events in your life.

EVENT	YEAR
I was born in Haiti.	*1981*

Make a timeline of the events in your life.

Former Senators Ben Nighthorse Campbell and Bob Dole

1951–53   **1957**   **1960**

←————|——————————|————|————————

*was in the
Air Force,
got his GED*

*moved to
Tokyo, Japan*

_____

_____

_____

Campbell on a motorcycle in front of the U.S. Capitol

Biography: Former U.S. Senator Ben Nighthorse Campbell

U.S. Senator Ben Nighthorse Campbell <u>was born in</u> Auburn, California on April 13, <u>1933</u>. His mother was a Portuguese immigrant, and his father was a Northern Cheyenne Indian.

As a child, Campbell liked sports, but he didn't like school. He didn't graduate from high school. Instead, in 1951, he joined the U.S. Air Force. While he was in the Air Force, he spent time in Korea, got his GED, and was promoted to Airman 2nd Class.

In 1953 Campbell left the Air Force and went to college. He graduated from San Jose University in 1957

and then, three years later, he moved to Tokyo, Japan. He studied at Meiji University and took judo lessons. In 1964, Campbell participated in the Olympic Games as a member of the U.S. Olympic Judo Team. Two years later, he married Linda Price and they had two children.

Campbell started his own business as a jewelry designer and judo instructor. Then, in 1992, Campbell became a U.S. senator from the state of Colorado. He served two terms as senator and retired at the end of his term in 2004 to live on his ranch with his family.

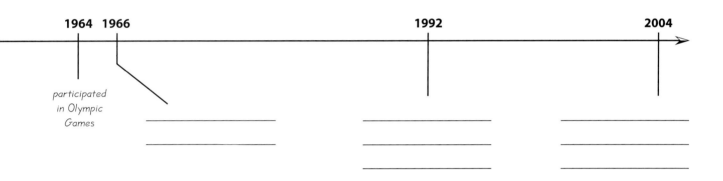

1964 1966   1992   2004

participated in Olympic Games

WINDOW ON MATH
Word Problems

 Read the information.

To solve a word problem, identify the important information. In the example below, the important information is underlined. Read the example and answer the question.

EXAMPLE: U.S. senators serve six-year terms. <u>Each state</u> in the U.S. has <u>two senators</u> and there are <u>50 states</u> in the U.S.

<u>How many senators</u> are there in the U.S. Senate?

 Read the word problem and underline the important information. Then solve the problem.

The citizens of each state elect, or choose, their two U.S. senators. Senators serve six-year terms. If a senator serves three terms, how many years is he or she a senator?

5 LESSON

How did you do it?

1 Practice the Conversation: Giving Advice 🎧

Listen to the conversation. Then listen and repeat.

A: Are you going to take a writing course next term ?

B: Do you think I need to take one ?

A: If you want to get your GED , I think you do.

Practice the conversation with a partner. Use these items.

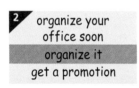
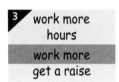

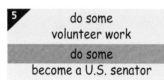

1	vote in the next election	2	organize your office soon
	vote		organize it
	be a good citizen		get a promotion

3	work more hours	4	go back to school	5	do some volunteer work
	work more		go back		do some
	get a raise		get a job		become a U.S. senator

2 Practice the Conversation: Asking for Advice 🎧

Listen to the conversation. Then listen and repeat.

A: You look happy. What's up?

B: I just got a raise .

A: That's great. I want to get a raise , too. How did you do it?

B: I worked hard and was always on time .

A: That's good advice.

Practice the conversation with a partner. Use these ideas.

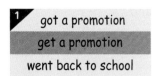
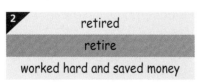
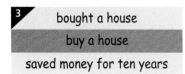

1	got a promotion	2	retired
	get a promotion		retire
	went back to school		worked hard and saved money

3	bought a house	4	started my own business	5	
	buy a house		start my own business		
	saved money for ten years		took some business classes		

60

3 Listen and Write: Listening to a Recorded Message 🎧

Listen and write the missing words. Then listen and check your answers.

Welcome to Westville Adult School. For information about Adult ESL

classes, press 1. For information about _____ _____, press 2.

For information about _____ _____, press 3.

To register for _____ _____, press 4.

To hear this message again, press _____ .

WINDOW ON PRONUNCIATION 🎧
Past Tense Endings

 Listen to the words. Then listen and repeat.

1. married	4. relaxed	7. cashed	10. studied	13. divorced
2. wanted	5. liked	8. deposited	11. graduated	14. used
3. moved	6. helped	9. immigrated	12. learned	15. promoted

 Write the words in the correct place in the chart.

Ending sounds like *t*	Ending sounds like *d*	Ending sounds like *id*
1. *relaxed*	1. *married*	1. *wanted*
2.	2.	2.
3.	3.	3.
4.	4.	4.
5.	5.	5.

 Complete the rules.

1. If the word ends in a *voiceless* consonant sound (*ck, k, f, p, ch, sh, s, x*), the past tense ending (*ed*) sounds like _____.
2. If the word ends in a *voiced* consonant sound (*b, g, j, m, n, r, z*) or a vowel sound, the past tense ending (*ed*) sounds like _____.
3. If the word ends in a *t* or *d* sound, the past tense ending (*ed*) sounds like _____.

 Work with a partner. Ask and answer the questions. Use complete sentences.

1. What did you like to do when you were a child?
2. What kind of job did you want when you were young?
3. What was the best thing you learned in school as a child?

School Calendar

1 Number the Events

Read the calendar. Put the events in order from first (1) to last (6).

_____ Semester ends

_____ Academic classes begin

__1__ New student registration

_____ Graduation

_____ Final exam period

_____ GED and Adult ESL classes begin

College students walking to class

Academic Calendar for Central Community College 2005
Spring Semester

New Student Registration
Dec. 6–Jan. 7

Classes Begin (GED, Adult ESL)
Jan. 8

Martin Luther King, Jr. Holiday
Jan. 17

Classes Begin (Academic Programs)
Jan. 18

Spring Break — No Classes
Mar. 5–Mar. 11

Spring Holiday
Mar. 25

Final Exam Period
May 4–May 10

Semester Ends
May 10

Graduation
May 11

Central Community College is closed on the holidays listed above.
Call (619) 555-3000 for more information. You can register in person, online, or over the telephone.

2 Read and Take Notes

Read the calendar on page 62 again and take notes.

What happens _____ ?	Event
on January 8	*GED and ESL classes begin*
on January 17	_____
from March 5 to March 11	_____
on May 11	_____
from May 4 to May 10	_____

When is _____ ?	Date
new student registration	_____
Martin Luther King, Jr. holiday	_____
graduation	_____

3 Write

Complete the registration form with your information.

Student registering for college class

Central Community College Student Registration Form

Last Name _____

First Name _____

Address _____

City _____

Birth Date _____ / _____ / _____

Sex ❑ Male   ❑ Female

What is your main goal at Central Community College?

❑ Take classes; don't plan to graduate

❑ Earn a GED

❑ Graduate from two-year college program

I plan to begin classes:

❑ Fall   ❑ Spring   Year: _____

Call (619) 555-3000 for more information.
You can register in person, online, or over the telephone.

63

7
LESSON

What do you know?

1 Listening Review 🎧

Listen and choose the best answer. Use the Answer Sheet.

1. A. That's great.
   B. I'm sorry.
   C. I can't.

3. A. Great! Where?
   B. Thank you.
   C. I don't think so.

2. A. That's too bad.
   B. That's good news.
   C. Fine, thank you.

4. A. I'm very sorry.
   B. Thanks a lot.
   C. Lucky you!

Listen to the conversations and choose the correct answer. Use the Answer Sheet.

5. A. an English class
   B. a business class
   C. a computer class

7. A. 1
   B. 2
   C. 3

6. A. to get more money
   B. to find a job
   C. to change jobs

8. A. work
   B. school
   C. the weekend

	ANSWER SHEET		
1	A	B	C
2	A	B	C
3	A	B	C
4	A	B	C
5	A	B	C
6	A	B	C
7	A	B	C
8	A	B	C
9	A	B	C
10	A	B	C

Listen and choose the sentence with the same meaning. Use the Answer Sheet.

9. A. She got a new shift.
   B. She got a promotion.
   C. She started a business.

10. A. He's lazy.
   B. He's disorganized.
   C. He's hardworking.

2 Dictation 🎧

Listen and write the sentences you hear.

1. _____

_____

2. _____

_____

3. _____

_____

3 Conversation Check: Pair Work

Student A: Go to page 165.

Student B: Ask your partner questions to complete this chart.

EXAMPLE: **B:** What are Sandy's personal goals?

A: She wants to get married.

First Name	Personal	GOALS Academic	Work
1. Sandy	get married	graduate from college	
2. Michael	buy a house		get a raise
3. Latisha	be a good parent		
4. Mani		get good grades	get a job
5. Zayda		get vocational training	get a promotion

✔

How many questions did you ask your partner?	How many questions did you answer?
☐ 1 ☐ 2 ☐ 3 ☐ 4 ☐ 5 ☐ 6 ☐ 7	☐ 1 ☐ 2 ☐ 3 ☐ 4 ☐ 5 ☐ 6 ☐ 7 ☐ 8

✔ LEARNING LOG

I know these words:

- ☐ bad attitude
- ☐ be a good citizen
- ☐ be a good parent
- ☐ become a U.S. citizen
- ☐ bookkeeper
- ☐ buy a house
- ☐ designer
- ☐ disorganized
- ☐ do volunteer work
- ☐ get a GED
- ☐ get a job

- ☐ get a promotion
- ☐ get a raise
- ☐ get good grades
- ☐ get married
- ☐ get vocational training
- ☐ go back to school
- ☐ good attitude
- ☐ good with people
- ☐ graduate from a university
- ☐ hardworking

- ☐ late
- ☐ lazy
- ☐ learn more English
- ☐ learn something new
- ☐ learn to use a computer
- ☐ mechanic
- ☐ office manager
- ☐ office worker
- ☐ on time
- ☐ organized
- ☐ read to your children

- ☐ salesperson
- ☐ save money
- ☐ senator
- ☐ spend time with your children
- ☐ start a business
- ☐ supervisor
- ☐ take a business course
- ☐ take a writing course
- ☐ vote

I can ask:
- ☐ What's up?
- ☐ How did you do it?
- ☐ Do you think I need to take a writing course?
- ☐ Who is going to get the job?

I can say:
- ☐ If you want to buy a house, you should save your money.
- ☐ I want to start my own business.
- ☐ I am going to take a writing course next year.

I can write:
- ☐ a list of goals
- ☐ information on a timeline
- ☐ information from a recorded message
- ☐ about a sequence of events

Spotlight: Writing

1 Read the story. Number the pictures from first (1) to last (6). Then complete the timeline.

AN IMPORTANT EVENT IN MY LIFE

by *James St. Fleur*

An important event in my life was on December 22, 1990. That's when my second son was born in Miami. I didn't watch when my older children were born. In Haiti, the father can't go into the hospital delivery room.

My wife started labor very early in the morning. I drove my wife to the hospital and the nurses put her in a room. Over the next few hours, they checked on her several times. Finally, they asked me to put on a hospital gown, and they took my wife and me to the delivery room. In less than an hour the baby came. The doctor gave me a pair of scissors and I cut the baby's umbilical cord. Then I held my son for the first time. I was very excited to see how my baby came into the world.

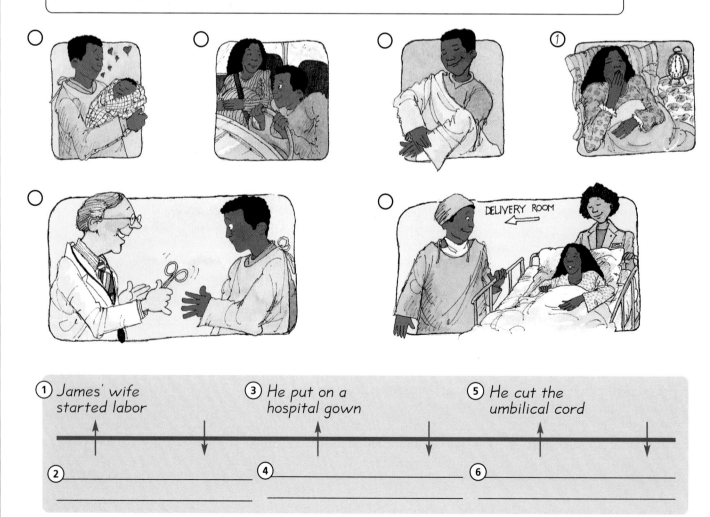

① James' wife started labor

③ He put on a hospital gown

⑤ He cut the umbilical cord

② _____

④ _____

⑥ _____

2 Underline the time words and phrases in the story below.

An important event in my life was <u>on March 12, 2002</u>. That's when I arrived in the United States.

My trip began in Vietnam in December 2001. We left our home in the mountains, and for several days we traveled to Cambodia. For three months, we stayed with relatives in Cambodia. Finally, we got our airplane tickets and left for California. I couldn't believe it.

FOCUS ON WRITING: Time Words

Time words and phrases help readers follow the events in a story.

Examples:

- An important event in my life was <u>on December 22, 1990</u>.
- My wife started labor <u>very early in the morning</u>.
- <u>Over the next few hours</u>, they checked on her several times.
- <u>Finally</u>, they asked me to put on a hospital gown.
- <u>In less than an hour</u>, the baby came.

3 Choose an important event in your life. Make a timeline with information about the event. Then write about the event. Use time words and phrases in your story.

→

_____

_____

_____

_____

_____

_____

_____

_____

_____

_____

_____

_____

_____

_____

_____

_____

LESSON 1

Do you have a heavy coat?

THINGS TO DO

1 Learn New Words 🎧

Look at the pictures. Listen to the words. Then listen and repeat.

① pair of athletic shoes
② jacket
③ heavy coat
④ pair of boots
⑤ coffeemaker
⑥ blender
⑦ toaster
⑧ can opener
⑨ peeler
⑩ cutting board
⑪ dish soap
⑫ broom
⑬ mop
⑭ bucket
⑮ vacuum

Which words are new to you? Circle them.

2 Write

Group the words in Activity 1. Write them in the chart below.

I HAVE	I DON'T HAVE	I WANT TO BUY

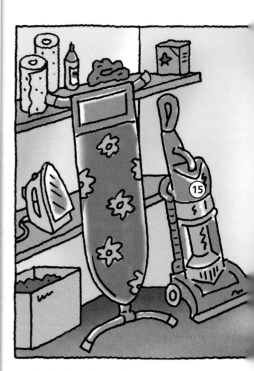

3 Find Someone Who

Talk to different classmates. Find someone who answers yes to your question. Write the person's name and the store information.

> EXAMPLE:
> A: Do you have a heavy coat?
> B: Yes, I do.
>
> A: Where did you buy it?
> B: I bought it at May's.

FIND SOMEONE WHO HAS _____	NAME	WHERE DID YOU BUY IT?
a jacket	_____	_____
a coffeemaker	_____	_____
a can opener	_____	_____
a blender	_____	_____
a vacuum	_____	_____
a broom	_____	_____

★ ★ ★ ★ ★ ★ ★ ★ ★ ★ ★ ★ ★ ★

TRY THIS Answer the questions below. Then tell a classmate.

What was the last thing you bought? Where did you buy it? Why did you buy it?

★ ★ ★ ★ ★ ★ ★ ★ ★ ★ ★ ★ ★ ★

Clothing

Kitchen Equipment

Cleaning Supplies

WINDOW ON GRAMMAR
Comparatives

A Read the sentences.

A broom is **cheaper** than a vacuum.
A coat is usually **more expensive** than a jacket.

ADJECTIVE	COMPARATIVE	ADJECTIVE	COMPARATIVE
cheap → cheaper		expensive → more expensive	
small → smaller		useful → more useful	
big → bigger		good → better	
nice → nicer		bad → worse	

B Complete the questions with a comparative from the list above. Then ask a classmate the questions.

1. Is a broom _____ than a mop?

2. Are boots _____ than shoes?

3. Is a toaster _____ than a blender?

4. Is a blender _____ than a can opener?

2 LESSON

Where do you buy shoes?

THINGS TO DO

1 Learn New Words 🎧

Look at the picture. Listen to the words. Then listen and repeat.

1. carry
2. take a break
3. go out of business
4. jewelry store
5. go into
6. toy store
7. push a stroller
8. furniture store
9. sale
10. demonstrate
11. mall directory
12. appliance store

Which words are new to you? Circle them.

2 Talk About the Picture

Write 3 true and 3 false statements about the picture. Read your sentences to the class. Your classmates can identify the false statements.

EXAMPLE: A: Gina bought something at the shoe store.
B: That's true.

A: Stoves are on sale at Sam's.
B: That's false.

3 Practice the Conversation 🎧

Listen to the conversation. Then listen and repeat.

A: Where do you buy shoes ?

B: I like May's Department Store.

A: Is May's better than Arches ?

B: I think so. It has a bigger selection .

Practice the conversation with a partner. Ask about these things.

1 appliances	2 toys	3 jewelry
Sam's	Jingle's	Gemma's
is cheaper	has a bigger selection	has better sales

4 furniture	5 books	6
Ben's	Pages	
has nicer furniture	has nicer salespeople	

70

3 LESSON

I saved seven dollars.

THINGS TO DO

1 Learn New Words 🎧

Look at the pictures. Listen to the words. Then listen and repeat.

① regular price   ③ half price
② 20 percent off   ④ marked down 50 percent

2 Compare

Read the sale ads and figure out the savings for each item.

Al's Superstore

Item	Regular Price	Sale Price	Savings
coffeemakers	$24.99	$17.99	$7.00
winter coats	_____	_____	_____
vacuums	_____	_____	_____

Barb's Discount House

Item	Regular Price	Sale Price	Savings
coffeemakers	_____	_____	_____
winter coats	_____	_____	_____
vacuums	_____	_____	_____

Where would you buy each item? Why?

3 Practice the Conversation 🎧

Listen to the conversation. Then listen and repeat.

A: Did you get a new coffeemaker ?

B: Yes. I got one on sale at Al's .

A: Really? Did you get a good deal?

B: I think so. I saved seven dollars .

Practice the conversation with a partner. Ask about these things.

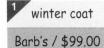
1 winter coat
Barb's / $99.00

2 vacuum
Al's / $34.99

3 coffeemaker
Barb's / ?

4

Man and woman window shopping

★ ★ ★ ★ ★ ★ ★ ★ ★ ★ ★ ★ ★ ★
TRY THIS Look at a newspaper. Find 2 sale ads and compare the prices. Where would you shop? Tell your classmates about the sales.
★ ★ ★ ★ ★ ★ ★ ★ ★ ★ ★ ★ ★ ★

AL'S SUPERSTORE

SUPER SATURDAY
January 24 8am-10pm

COFFEEMAKERS
ON SALE ①
Reg. **$24.99**
SALE **$17.99**

STOREWIDE SALE!!!

WHIRLY BAGLESS UPRIGHT VACUUM
Reg. **$69.98**
SALE **$34.99** ④

ENTIRE STOCK MARKED DOWN 50%

GOLD STAR CLEARANCE

70% OFF ALL WINTER COATS
Reg. **$125.00**
Now **$37.50**

BARB'S DISCOUNT HOUSE

Ovay coffeemakers
Now 20% off
reg. $28.99
sale price
$23.19 ②

All Winter Coats
½ PRICE! ③
Reg. $198.00
Now $99.00

CLEARANCE SALE
All Hadley vacuums must go!
Now reduced 30%
Were $149.98
Now $104.99

OPEN MON. – SAT. 9AM – 9PM, SUN. 9AM – 6PM

WINDOW ON MATH
Percentages

A Read the sentences.

1. 10% (ten percent) = 10/100 (ten over one hundred) = .10 (point ten)
2. Ten percent of fifty dollars equals five dollars.
3. 50% (fifty percent) = 50/100 (fifty over one hundred) = .50 (point fifty)
4. Fifty percent of fifty dollars equals twenty-five dollars.

B Answer the questions.

1. A $200.00 coat is marked down 50%. How much does it cost?
2. A $50.00 coffeemaker is 10% off. How much does it cost?
3. A $100.00 vacuum is 70% off. How much does it cost?

73

4 LESSON

A Shopper's Calendar

THINGS TO DO

1 Preview

Scan the article. Which of the things below can you learn from it? Check (✓) your answers.

☐ when things are on sale

☐ which stores are cheaper

☐ how much appliances cost

☐ what you should buy in the winter

2 Read and Take Notes

Read the article and take notes in the chart below.

ITEM	THE BEST TIME TO BUY
summer clothes	*in September*
outdoor furniture	
fall clothes	
stereos	
spring clothes	
sheets and towels	
televisions	

3 Write

Look in a newspaper for information about sales in your area. Then write about the sales that interest you.

> EXAMPLE: It's February now, and a lot of things are on sale. At Leblanc's True Value Hardware store, everything is 10–70% off. At Fortunes, winter clothes are on sale. On February 6 and 7, you can get an extra 20% off already marked-down clothes.

★ ★

 TRY THIS Use the Internet to shop for sales. Go online and look for a store you know. Find the sale section on the store's web site. Choose one item. Tell your classmates the original price and the sale price.

★ ★

JANUARY

Go shopping in January for the last of the fall clothing. Leftovers from the December holidays are also marked down now. There are also sales on sheets and towels.

APRIL

Spring clothes first go on sale in April. However, final markdowns are months away.

JUNE AND JULY

Father's Day is a good time to shop for consumer electronics.

On sale are:

- DVD players
- stereos
- home computers
- CD players
- televisions
- PDAs

A Shopper's Calendar:
Save Money All Year

In September, it's time for back-to-school shopping. Parents take their children to the mall to buy new clothes for school. But what are the smartest shoppers buying? They are buying summer clothes. Smart shoppers know that "off season" clothes are 60–80% less than the original price. As the seasons change, so do the items on sale. Here's what's for sale at different times during the year:

AUGUST

This is the time for final markdowns on spring clothes.

OCTOBER

The first big sales of fall clothing begin in October. But don't get too excited. Prices will get a lot cheaper in January.

SEPTEMBER

At the end of the summer, garden supplies go on sale. This is a good time to buy plants and outdoor furniture.

WINDOW ON GRAMMAR
Superlatives

A Read the sentences.

<u>The best</u> time to buy sheets is in January.
<u>The worst</u> time to buy garden supplies is in the spring.

ADJECTIVE	COMPARATIVE	SUPERLATIVE
good →	better →	the best
bad →	worse →	the worst
cheap →	cheaper →	the cheapest
expensive →	more expensive →	the most expensive

B Complete the sentences.

1. Fall clothes are the _____ in January.

2. September is the _____ time to buy plants.

3. April is a _____ time to buy spring clothes, but August is the _____ time.

75

I want to return this.

1 Practice the Conversation: Exchanging Something 🎧

Listen to the conversation. Then listen and repeat.

A: Can I help you?

B: Yes. I want to return this jacket .

A: Okay. Was there something wrong with it?

B: Yes. It's too tight .

A: Do you want to exchange it for a looser one ?

B: Yes, I do.

A: Okay. I'll be right with you.

Practice the conversation with a partner. Use these items.

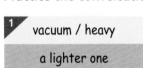

1 vacuum / heavy — a lighter one

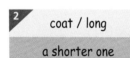

2 coat / long — a shorter one

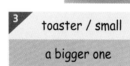

3 toaster / small — a bigger one

4

2 Practice the Conversation: Asking for a Refund 🎧

Listen to the conversation. Then listen and repeat.

A: Can I help you?

B: Yes, I want to return these toys . They're just too noisy .

A: Do you want some quieter ones?

B: No, thank you. I just want a refund.

A: Do you have your receipt?

B: Yes, I have it right here.

Practice the conversation with a partner. Use these items.

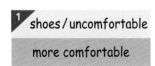

1 shoes / uncomfortable — more comfortable

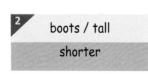

2 boots / tall — shorter

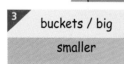

3 buckets / big — smaller

4

3 Practice the Conversation: Comparing Price and Quality 🎧

Listen to the conversation. Then listen and repeat.

A: Which coat do you like better?

B: This one. It's much softer .

A: Yes, and it's a lot more expensive, too.

B: How much more expensive?

A: Fifty dollars .

B: It is a little nicer, but fifty dollars is a lot more
    expensive. I'd get the other one.

Practice the conversation with a partner.
Use these items.

1 jacket	**2** toaster oven	**3** vacuum
more attractive	bigger	easier to use
$200.00	$30.00	$100.00
$200.00	$30.00	$100.00

4

WINDOW ON PRONUNCIATION 🎧
Stress

A Listen to the conversations. Then listen and repeat.

1. A: What's wrong with it?
   B: It's too tight.

2. A: Is it tight enough?
   B: It's too tight.

3. A: How is that one?
   B: It's much softer.

4. A: Is it softer?
   B: Yes, it's much softer.

Listen to the conversations again. Circle the stressed words.

B Work with a partner. Practice the conversations. Stress
the important words. Circle the stressed word in each
conversation.

1. A: What's wrong with it?
   B: It's too small.

2. A: Is it a heavy coat?
   B: Yes, it's too heavy.

3. A: Is this one quieter?
   B: It's much quieter.

4. A: Why do you like that one?
   B: It's much cheaper.

Shopping Tips

1 Check *True* or *False*

Read the shopping tips on page 79. Then look at the statements below and check (✓) *True* or *False*.

	True	False
1. You can find store coupons in the newspaper.	☐	☐
2. To use a store coupon, you should mail it to the store.	☐	☐
3. You can use a store coupon after you make your purchase.	☐	☐
4. You pay extra for something when you use a layaway plan.	☐	☐
5. When you put something on layaway, you can't take it home with you right away.	☐	☐
6. A warranty tells how much you paid for something.	☐	☐
7. When you have a problem with a purchase, you should call the store where you bought it.	☐	☐

2 Think About It

Answer the questions below. Use the information in Sam's Layaway Plan and the information on page 79.

1. Sara wants to buy a $120.00 vacuum at Sam's Store, but she doesn't have enough money to pay for it now. She decides to use the store layaway plan. How much money does she need to put down?

   _____

2. Tim bought a new Shark washing machine for $600.00. After six months, the machine stopped working. What should Tim do?

   _____

   _____

> ## SAM'S
> ### LAYAWAY PLAN
> ❶ **Make a 20% deposit.**
> ❷ **Full payment required in 3 months**

3. Dana is looking for a new coat and an electric coffeemaker. From the newspaper, she cut out two bonus coupons for May's Department Store. At May's, she found an $80.00 coat marked down to $50.00. She also found a coffeemaker on sale for $30.00. With the coupons, how much will she pay for the coat and the coffeemaker?

   _____

★ ★

TRY THIS   Think about something you do to save money when you are shopping. Then write your shopping tip and share it with your classmates.

★ ★

Tips From Smart Shoppers

Tip #1 Use Store Coupons

You can save money by cutting coupons from newspapers and store flyers. Just give the coupons to the cashier when you make your purchase, and you'll get a discount. Keep these things in mind when you use coupons:

- Check the date on the coupon. Most coupons are valid, or good, for a short period of time.
- Stores use coupons to get you to buy something you don't really need.

STOREWIDE BONUS COUPON
EXTRA **15%** OFF
VALID FRIDAY AND SATURDAY
JUNE 6 & 7
MAY'S DEPARTMENT STORE
NO DISCOUNT on jewelry or cosmetics.

Tip #2 Use Layaway

Many stores have layaway plans. You make a deposit or down payment, and you have a certain amount of time to complete your payment. The store keeps the item until you pay in full. Usually there is no extra fee or service charge.

Tip #3 Read the Warranty

A warranty or guarantee tells what a company will do if you have a problem with something you buy. It's especially important to read the warranty before you buy something expensive. You should also save the warranty and any packaging your purchase came in.

SHARK® Washing Machine Warranty

Full One-Year Warranty

For one (1) year from the date of original retail purchase, any part that fails in normal home use will be repaired or replaced free of charge.

To Receive Warranty Service

Call Shark Customer Service toll-free at 1-555-456-4566. You will need the model and serial numbers of your appliance, the name and address of the dealer, and the date of purchase.

LESSON 7

What do you know?

1 Listening Review 🎧

Listen and choose the correct answer. Use the Answer Sheet.

1. A. It was on sale.
   B. I save ten dollars.
   C. at May's Department Store

2. A. the boots
   B. the coat
   C. the stereo

3. A. Yes, I went to the shoe store.
   B. Yes, it was on sale.
   C. Yes, I bought a new coat.

4. A. in June
   B. last year
   C. at the appliance store

5. A. Yes, they are. They're half price.
   B. Yes, they are. They are very useful.
   C. Yes, there is. It's a storewide sale.

6. A. Yes, it was heavy.
   B. Yes, it was very expensive.
   C. Yes, it was very cheap.

7. A. at Sam's Appliance Store
   B. at Gemma's Jewelry Store
   C. at Ben's Furniture Store

8. A. I like it better.
   B. It has better sales.
   C. It's better.

9. A. He's carrying a bucket.
   B. He's wearing a coat.
   C. He's going into a store.

10. A. They are 50 percent off.
    B. vacuums and coffeemakers
    C. It's the regular price.

ANSWER SHEET			
1	A	B	C
2	A	B	C
3	A	B	C
4	A	B	C
5	A	B	C
6	A	B	C
7	A	B	C
8	A	B	C
9	A	B	C
10	A	B	C

2 Dictation 🎧

Listen and write the sentences you hear.

1. _____

   _____

2. _____

   _____

3 Conversation Check: Pair Work

Student A: Go to page 166.

Student B: Ask your partner questions to complete this chart.

EXAMPLE:
B: What's on sale at Terry's?
A: Vacuums.
B: How much are they?
A: They're 10 percent off.

Lou's Discount House		Terry's Superstore	
What's on sale?	**How much?**	**What's on sale?**	**How much?**
blenders	20% off	vacuums	10% off
toaster ovens	1/2 price		
brooms	30% off		
cutting boards	50% off		

✔

How many questions did you ask your partner?	How many questions did you answer?
☐ 1 ☐ 2 ☐ 3 ☐ 4 ☐ 5 ☐ 6 ☐ 7 ☐ 8	☐ 1 ☐ 2 ☐ 3 ☐ 4 ☐ 5 ☐ 6 ☐ 7 ☐ 8

✔ LEARNING LOG

I know these words:

- ☐ appliance store
- ☐ blender
- ☐ broom
- ☐ bucket
- ☐ can opener
- ☐ carry
- ☐ coffeemaker
- ☐ cutting board

- ☐ demonstrate
- ☐ dish soap
- ☐ furniture store
- ☐ go into
- ☐ go out of business
- ☐ half price
- ☐ heavy coat
- ☐ jacket

- ☐ jewelry store
- ☐ mall directory
- ☐ marked down
- ☐ mop
- ☐ pair of athletic shoes
- ☐ pair of boots
- ☐ peeler
- ☐ push a stroller

- ☐ regular price
- ☐ sale
- ☐ take a break
- ☐ toaster
- ☐ toy store
- ☐ twenty percent off
- ☐ vacuum

I can ask:

- ☐ Where did you buy it?
- ☐ Where do you buy shoes?
- ☐ Which store is better?
- ☐ Which store has better sales?
- ☐ Did you get a good deal?

I can say:

- ☐ I got it on sale.
- ☐ I saved seven dollars.
- ☐ It's marked down 50%.
- ☐ The best time to buy sheets is in January.
- ☐ I want to return this jacket.
- ☐ I just want a refund.

I can write:

- ☐ sentences comparing two things
- ☐ a price comparison chart
- ☐ notes about a reading
- ☐ shopping tips

81

Spotlight: Grammar

COMPARATIVE FORMS OF ADJECTIVES	
One-Syllable Adjectives	**Two-Syllable Adjectives**

One-Syllable Adjectives

- Add *-er* to most one-syllable adjectives.

  EXAMPLES:

  cheap ⟶ cheaper   tall ⟶ taller
  safe ⟶ safer   short ⟶ shorter
  sick ⟶ sicker   old ⟶ older

- For one-syllable adjectives that end in a single vowel and a consonant, double the consonant and add *-er.*

  EXAMPLES:

  hot ⟶ hotter   fat ⟶ fatter
  sad ⟶ sadder   fit ⟶ fitter

Two-Syllable Adjectives

- For two-syllable adjectives that end in *-y,* change the *-y* to *-i* and add *-er.*

  EXAMPLES:

  happy ⟶ happier
  funny ⟶ funnier

- Use the word *more* with most two-syllable adjectives.

  EXAMPLES:

  beautiful ⟶ more beautiful
  athletic ⟶ more athletic
  famous ⟶ more famous

Irregular Adjectives
- These adjectives have an irregular comparative form.

  good ⟶ better
  bad ⟶ worse
  far ⟶ farther

1 Use the information in the box above. Write the comparative form of each adjective.

Adjective	Comparative		Adjective	Comparative		Adjective	Comparative
1. pretty	*prettier*		5. exciting	_____		9. curly	_____
2. new	_____		6. tight	_____		10. slim	_____
3. nervous	_____		7. loose	_____		11. intelligent	_____
4. big	_____		8. heavy	_____		12. angry	_____

2 Choose a word to complete each of the following conversations. (More than one answer may be possible.) Then practice the conversations with a partner.

1. A: Why did they mail a money order instead of cash?

   B: Because a money order is _____.

2. A: Why did you decide to go to Florida instead of New York?

   B: Because Florida is _____.

3. A: Why did she marry Jim instead of Tim?

   B: Because Jim is _____.

4. A: Why did they go to May's instead of Sam's?

   B: Because May's is _____.

5. A: Why did they use layaway instead of a credit card?

   B: Because layaway is _____.

SUPERLATIVE FORMS OF ADJECTIVES

One-Syllable Adjectives	*Two-Syllable Adjectives*
• Add -*est* to most one-syllable adjectives. EXAMPLES: cheap → the cheapest tall → the tallest safe → the safest short → the shortest sick → the sickest old → the oldest • For one-syllable adjectives that end in a single vowel and a consonant, double the consonant and add -*est*. EXAMPLES: hot → the hottest fat → the fattest sad → the saddest fit → the fittest	• For two-syllable adjectives that end in -*y*, change the -*y* to -*i* and add -*est*. EXAMPLES: happy → the happiest funny → the funniest • Use the word *most* with most adjectives with two or more syllables. EXAMPLES: beautiful → the most beautiful athletic → the most athletic famous → the most famous *Irregular Adjectives* • These adjectives have an irregular superlative form. good → the best bad → the worst far → the farthest

3 Use the information in the box above. Write the superlative form of each adjective.

Adjective	Superlative		Adjective	Superlative
1. pretty	*the prettiest*		7. loose	_____
2. new	_____		8. heavy	_____
3. nervous	_____		9. curly	_____
4. big	_____		10. slim	_____
5. exciting	_____		11. intelligent	_____
6. tight	_____		12. angry	_____

4 Complete the questions with *the* and the superlative form of the adjectives in parentheses. Then ask a classmate the questions.

1. Who is _____ *the oldest* _____ person in your family? (old)

2. What is _____ city you ever visited? (nice)

3. When did you feel _____? (nervous)

4. What was _____ thing you bought last month? (expensive)

5. Who is _____ person you know? (funny)

6. What is _____ city in the world? (large)

7. When is _____ time to buy electronics? (good)

8. What is _____ way to get to Europe? (fast)

Did you eat any fish yesterday?

THINGS TO DO

1 Learn New Words 🎧

Look at the pictures. Listen to the words. Then listen and repeat.

① red meat
② poultry
③ fish
④ eggs
⑤ milk
⑥ ice cream
⑦ cheese
⑧ oil
⑨ fruit
⑩ peanuts
⑪ vegetables
⑫ sugar
⑬ flour
⑭ cereal
⑮ soft drinks
⑯ coffee

Which words are new to you? Circle them.

2 Check *True* or *False*

Study the bar graph and read the sentences below. Check (✓) *True* or *False*. Then correct the false sentences.

	True	False
1. Americans eat about 325 pounds of fruit a year.	☐	☐
2. Americans eat 50 pounds of vegetables a year.	☐	☐
3. Americans eat more red meat than poultry.	☐	☐
4. Americans eat more fruit than vegetables.	☐	☐
5. Americans drink about 10 pounds of coffee a year.	☐	☐

3 Interview

Work with a partner. Ask your partner the questions below. Record your partner's answers.

A: Did you eat any fish yesterday?

B: Yes, I did . I had fish for dinner .

A: Did you eat any eggs yesterday?

B: No, I didn't .

Did you eat any _____ yesterday?	Yes, I did. I had _____ for _____.				No, I didn't.
	breakfast	lunch	dinner	a snack	
fish	☐	☐	☐	☐	☐
red meat	☐	☐	☐	☐	☐
fruit	☐	☐	☐	☐	☐
vegetables	☐	☐	☐	☐	☐
_____	☐	☐	☐	☐	☐

pounds (y-axis label)

400
350
300
250 ——②
200
150
100
50
0

② (poultry image)

① (red meat image)

★ ★ ★ ★ ★ ★ ★ ★ ★ ★ ★ ★ ★ ★ ★ ★

TRY THIS Take notes on what you eat for one week. Multiply the amounts by 52 to estimate what you eat in one year. How do your numbers compare to the graph? Share your results with the class.

pounds (lbs.) of food	x 52
_2_ lbs. of fish	_104_ lbs.
____ lbs. of fruit	____ lbs.
____ lbs. of cheese	____ lbs.

EXAMPLE: I eat about 104 pounds of fish a year. I eat more fish than the average American.

★ ★ ★ ★ ★ ★ ★ ★ ★ ★ ★ ★ ★ ★ ★ ★

How much does the average person in the U.S. eat each year?

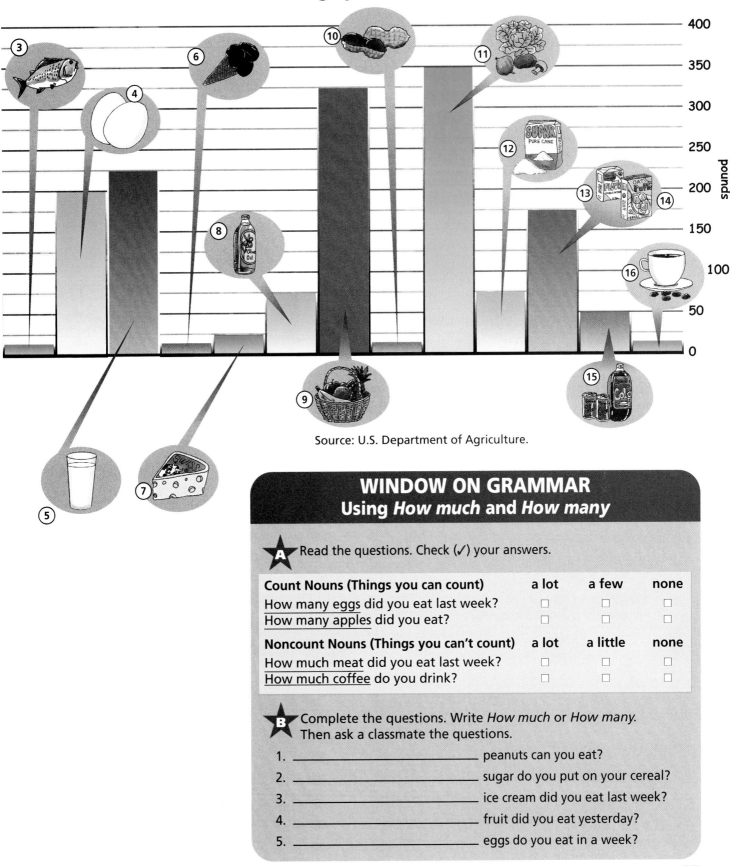

Source: U.S. Department of Agriculture.

WINDOW ON GRAMMAR
Using *How much* and *How many*

A Read the questions. Check (✓) your answers.

Count Nouns (Things you can count)	a lot	a few	none
How many eggs did you eat last week?	☐	☐	☐
How many apples did you eat?	☐	☐	☐

Noncount Nouns (Things you can't count)	a lot	a little	none
How much meat did you eat last week?	☐	☐	☐
How much coffee do you drink?	☐	☐	☐

B Complete the questions. Write *How much* or *How many*.
Then ask a classmate the questions.

1. _____ peanuts can you eat?
2. _____ sugar do you put on your cereal?
3. _____ ice cream did you eat last week?
4. _____ fruit did you eat yesterday?
5. _____ eggs do you eat in a week?

Can you bring me a menu, please?

THINGS TO DO

1 Learn New Words 🎧

Look at the picture. Listen to the words. Then listen and repeat.

1. counter
2. menu
3. waiter
4. check
5. booth
6. hostess
7. tray
8. plate
9. bowl
10. napkin
11. serve food
12. take an order
13. pour
14. trip over
15. fall off
16. set the table
17. clear the table
18. spill

Which words are new to you? Circle them.

2 Talk About the Picture

Write 5 questions about the picture. Then ask your classmates the questions.

EXAMPLES: How many people are in the restaurant?
What is the person behind Dot doing?

3 Practice the Conversation 🎧

Listen to the conversation. Then listen and repeat.

A: Excuse me.

B: Yes. Can I help you?

A: Yes. Can you bring me a menu , please?

B: Sure. I'll get one for you right away.

Practice the conversation with a partner. Ask about these things.

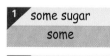
1. some sugar
   some

2. some water
   some

3. a napkin
   one

4. the check
   it

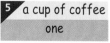
5. a cup of coffee
   one

6. 💡

★ ★

TRY THIS

Describe your favorite restaurant. Does it have booths? Is the food delicious? Are the waiters nice?

Lucy

Lisa

Janet

LESSON 3

Are you ready to order?

THINGS TO DO

1 Learn New Words 🎧

Look at the menu. Listen to the words. Then listen and repeat.

- ① appetizers
- ② soups
- ③ salads
- ④ main dishes
- ⑤ sandwiches
- ⑥ side orders
- ⑦ desserts
- ⑧ beverages

Write the words on the lines in the menu.

2 Practice the Conversation 🎧

Listen to the conversation. Then listen and repeat.

A: Are you ready to order?

B: Yes. I'd like a small onion soup and a chicken sandwich .

A: Do you want something to drink with your sandwich ?

B: Yes. I'd like some tea , please.

A: Large or small?

B: Small , please.

Practice the conversation. Ask about these things.

1 the fish stew and a side order of fries
your stew
a cup of tea / Large

2 the hamburger special and a small garden salad
your hamburger
an orange soda / Small

3 the stuffed mushrooms and a large vegetable soup
your soup
a root beer / Large

4

3 Interview

Interview a partner. Write your partner's answers.

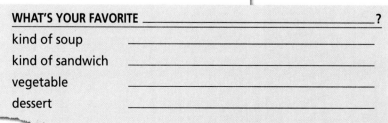

WHAT'S YOUR FAVORITE _____?

kind of soup _____

kind of sandwich _____

vegetable _____

dessert _____

Casa Alberto

① _____ Appetizers _____

STUFFED MUSHROOMS	5.25
SHRIMP COCKTAIL	4.75

② _____

ONION	Small 2.50	Large 3.50
CHICKEN	Small 1.75	Large 2.50
BLACK BEAN	Small 1.75	Large 2.50
VEGETABLE	Small 1.75	Large 2.50

③ _____

FRUIT SALAD	Small 2.50	Large 4.50
GARDEN SALAD	Small 2.00	Large 4.00

★ ★ ★ ★ ★ ★ ★ ★ ★ ★ ★ ★ ★ ★ ★ ★ ★ ★

TRY THIS Write a menu with your favorite foods and drinks. Write prices for each item. Share your menu with the class.

★ ★ ★ ★ ★ ★ ★ ★ ★ ★ ★ ★ ★ ★ ★ ★ ★ ★

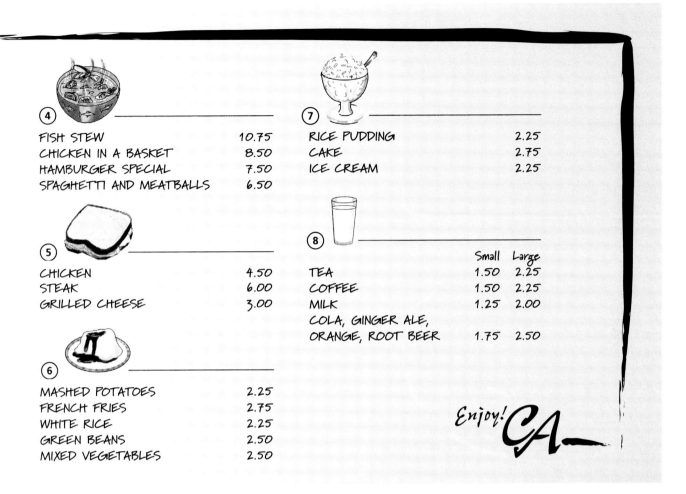

④		
FISH STEW	10.75	
CHICKEN IN A BASKET	8.50	
HAMBURGER SPECIAL	7.50	
SPAGHETTI AND MEATBALLS	6.50	

⑤

CHICKEN	4.50
STEAK	6.00
GRILLED CHEESE	3.00

⑥

MASHED POTATOES	2.25
FRENCH FRIES	2.75
WHITE RICE	2.25
GREEN BEANS	2.50
MIXED VEGETABLES	2.50

⑦

RICE PUDDING	2.25
CAKE	2.75
ICE CREAM	2.25

⑧

	Small	Large
TEA	1.50	2.25
COFFEE	1.50	2.25
MILK	1.25	2.00
COLA, GINGER ALE, ORANGE, ROOT BEER	1.75	2.50

Enjoy! CA

WINDOW ON MATH
Computing a Tip

A Read the meal receipt and explanation.

In many states, you pay a tax on food in a restaurant. It is often 5–8%. People usually pay a tip for service. It is often 15%. To compute the tip, multiply the total food cost, before tax, by 15%.
EXAMPLE: $7.00 x .15 = $1.05

Casa Alberto

total food:	$7.00
tax:	$0.35
tip:	$1.05
Total:	**$8.40**

Thank you!

B Complete the chart below.

Total food cost:	$16.00	$24.00	$32.00
5% tax:	_____	_____	_____
15% tip:	_____	_____	_____
Total cost of meal:	_____	_____	_____

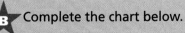

89

4 LESSON

Favorite Recipes

THINGS TO DO

1 Learn New Words 🎧

Look at the pictures. Listen to the words. Then listen and repeat.

1. fry
2. bake
3. boil
4. cut up
5. slice
6. mix
7. form a ball
8. roll
9. heat

Which words are new to you? Circle them.

2 Read and Number the Pictures

Read the recipe on page 91. Number the pictures below from first (1) to last (5).

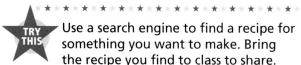

Use the pictures. Retell the instructions without looking at the recipe on page 91.

3 Write

Write the ingredients and instructions for a dish you like. Then share your recipe with the class.

⭐ **TRY THIS** Use a search engine to find a recipe for something you want to make. Bring the recipe you find to class to share.

| chocolate cake | **Search** |

Bola Bola

by Irma Magwil

Here is my recipe for Bola Bola. This dish is very popular in the Philippines. My husband loves to eat it. In English, this dish is called meatballs.

Ingredients

- *1 pound ground beef*
- *1 hot red pepper, cut up into small pieces*
- *3 eggs*
- *2 tablespoons spring onions, sliced*
- *2 tablespoons soy sauce*
- *1/3 cup white flour*
- *black pepper and salt to taste*
- *ketchup*
- *oil for frying*

Instructions

1. *Mix all the ingredients except for the flour, ketchup, and oil in a large bowl.*
2. *Take a spoonful of the mixture. Form it into a ball and roll it in the flour.*
3. *Heat some oil in a frying pan.*
4. *Fry the balls until they become golden brown.*
5. *Serve with ketchup (for dipping) and rice.*

ground beef

ketchup

spring onion

hot red pepper

WINDOW ON GRAMMAR
Quantity Words

A Study the pictures.

With quantity words, we can count noncount nouns.

slices   cups   pieces   glasses   pounds   bowls

B What did you eat and drink yesterday? Make a list, using quantity words. Then read your list to a classmate.

EXAMPLE: 2 cups of coffee, 2 pieces of fruit, 6 glasses of water, 4 small pieces of chicken, and a bowl of ice cream

91

5 LESSON

For here or to go?

1 Practice the Conversation: Placing a Food Order 🎧

Listen to the conversation. Then listen and repeat.

A: What can I get for you?

B: I'd like a large salad and a root beer .

A: What size root beer?

B: Large , please.

A: For here or to go?

B: For here .

Practice the conversation with a partner. Use these ideas.

1 a hamburger and some coffee	2 a cheeseburger and a salad	3 a chicken sandwich and some tea	4
coffee	salad	tea	
Small/To go	Small/For here	Large/To go	

2 Practice the Conversation: Computing the Cost of a Meal 🎧

Listen to the conversation. Then listen and repeat.

A: Can I help you?

B: Yes. I'd like a veggie sandwich and a root beer .

A: What size root beer ?

B: Small , please.

A: Do you want some fries with that?

B: No, thank you.

A: That will be $3.75 .

Practice the conversation with a partner. Use these ideas.

Burgers		Sandwiches	
Hamburger	2.10	Steak	3.50
Cheeseburger	2.40	Tuna Fish	3.25
Double Burger	3.20	Veggie	2.75
Side Orders		Salads	
French Fries	1.50 – 2.50	Garden	1.75 – 3.00
Onion Rings	2.00 – 3.00	Tuna	2.00 – 3.50

Beverages
Soft Drinks   1.00 – 1.50
    Root Beer, Cola, Diet Cola,
    Orange, Ginger Ale
Coffee & Tea 0.75 – 1.25

1 a hamburger and some coffee	2 a garden salad	3 a steak sandwich and an order of fries	4
coffee	salad	fries	
Large	Large	Small	
a salad	a sandwich	something to drink	
$3.35	$3.00	$5.00	

3 Listen and Write 🎧

Listen to 3 people ordering at a fast food restaurant. Check (✓) what each person orders.
Then write the total you hear for each order.

	Person #1	*Person #2*	*Person #3*
Sandwiches			
Steak	✓	☐	☐
Chicken	☐	☐	☐
Veggie	☐	☐	☐
Salads			
Garden	☐	☐	☐
Fruit	☐	☐	☐
Beverages			
Coffee	☐	☐	☐
Tea	☐	☐	☐
Orange soda	☐	☐	☐
Root beer	☐	☐	☐
Total	$_____	$_____	$_____

WINDOW ON PRONUNCIATION 🎧
Intonation Patterns in Sentences and Questions

 A Listen to the sentences. Then listen and repeat.

1. I'd like a large salad and a coffee.

2. I'd like a veggie sandwich, a salad and a root beer.

3. I'd like the onion soup, an order of fries, and a chicken sandwich.

4. For here or to go?

5. Large or small?

 B Listen to the conversations. Then listen and repeat.

1. Waiter: Do you want french fries or a salad?
   Customer: French fries.

2. Waiter: Do you want french fries or a salad?
   Customer: Sure. I'll take a salad.

3. Waiter: Would you like cake or ice cream?
   Customer: Cake, please.

4. Waiter: Would you like cake or ice cream?
   Customer: No, thanks. I'm too full.

 C Work with a partner. Take turns asking and answering the questions from Activity B.

The FDA and Food Labels

1 Read and Check *True* or *False*

Read the article and food label below. Read the sentences and check (✓) *True* or *False*.
Then correct the false statements.

	True	False
1. The Food and Drug Administration is a private agency.	☐	☐
2. The FDA inspects our food.	☐	☐
3. The FDA is not responsible for food labels.	☐	☐
4. All foods must have an ingredient list.	☐	☐
5. Tomatoes are the main ingredient in Mark's Pizza.	☐	☐
6. Tomato puree is made with tomato paste and onions.	☐	☐

The FDA and Food Labels

The Food and Drug Administration (FDA) is a government agency. The goal of the FDA is to keep our food and drugs safe. The FDA has over 9,000 employees including many scientists and food inspectors.

The FDA is responsible for the labels on food. The agency makes sure that food labels are truthful and that they provide useful information for consumers.

An ingredient list appears on any food with two or more ingredients. For example, pizza, soup, and ice cream each have an ingredient list. The ingredients always appear in descending order, by weight. In other words, the main ingredient appears first. In the example to the right, the main ingredient in Mark's Cheese Pizza is wheat flour.

INGREDIENTS: **CRUST:** WHEAT FLOUR WITH MALTED BARLEY FLOUR, WATER, PARTIALLY HYDROGENATED VEGETABLE OIL (SOYBEAN AND/OR COTTONSEED OIL) WITH SOY LECITHIN, ARTIFICIAL FLAVOR AND ARTIFICIAL COLOR (BETA CAROTENE), SOYBEAN OIL, YEAST, HIGH FRUCTOSE CORN SYRUP, SALT, CALCIUM PROPIONATE ADDED TO RETARD SPOILAGE OF CRUST, L-CYSTEINE MONOHYDROCHLORIDE; **SAUCE:** TOMATO PUREE (WATER, TOMATO PASTE), WATER, GREEN PEPPERS, SALT, LACTOSE AND FLAVORING, SPICES, FOOD STARCH – MODIFIED, SUGAR, CORN OIL, XANTHAN GUM, GARLIC POWDER; TOPPING: LOW MOISTURE PART SKIM MOZZARELLA CHEESE (PASTEURIZED MILK, CHEESE CULTURES, SALT, ENZYMES).

**Manufactured by Mark's Pizza,
Silver Spring, MD 20901**

2 Match

Match each list of ingredients to a food. Write the number of the food.

②　PEANUTS, SALT, CORNSTARCH, SUGAR, MONOSODIUM GLUTAMATE, YEAST, CORN SYRUP, PAPRIKA, HYDROLYZED SOY PROTEIN, NATURAL FLAVOR, GARLIC AND ONION POWDER

○　TOMATOES, TOMATO PUREE, ONION, RED PEPPER, VINEGAR, SUGAR, SALT, OLIVE OIL, GARLIC, BASIL, OREGANO, BLACK PEPPER, CITRIC ACID

○　ROLLED OATS, MARGARINE, SKIM MILK, SALT, SOY LECITHIN, BROWN SUGAR, WHEAT FLOUR, RAISINS, EGGS, BAKING SODA, VANILLA

○　TOMATOES, TOMATO JUICE, SEA SALT, CITRIC ACID, CALCIUM CHLORIDE

★　★　★　★　★　★　★　★　★　★　★　★　★　★　★　★　★　★

TRY THIS ★　Look at the label on 3 cans, boxes, or jars of food from a grocery store. For each food, list the 3 main ingredients. In class, read the ingredients for one of your foods aloud and ask your classmates to guess the food.

EXAMPLE: The three main ingredients for this food are: wheat flour, wheat meal, and honey. What's my food?

★　★　★　★　★　★　★　★　★　★　★　★　★　★　★　★　★　★

UNIT 6: Food

What do you know?

1 Listening Review 🎧

Listen and choose the correct answer. Use the Answer Sheet.

1. A. Yes, I did.
   B. Yes, she did.
   C. Yes, they did.

2. A. Yes, I had an egg.
   B. Yes, I had a hamburger.
   C. Yes, I had a banana.

3. A. three
   B. a little
   C. a few

4. A. A menu?
   B. A soft drink?
   C. A napkin?

5. A. Yes. I'd like a large salad.
   B. Large, please.
   C. No, that's all.

6. A. cake
   B. coffee
   C. shrimp cocktail

7. A. Yes, I'd like a chicken sandwich.
   B. Yes, I'd like a cup of coffee.
   C. Yes, I'd like a fruit salad.

8. A. Yes, I'd like the vegetable soup.
   B. Yes, I'd like some ice cream.
   C. Yes, I'd like some mixed vegetables.

9. A. coffee
   B. cereal
   C. eggs

10. A. I like them.
    B. I bake them.
    C. A lot.

	ANSWER SHEET		
1	Ⓐ	Ⓑ	Ⓒ
2	Ⓐ	Ⓑ	Ⓒ
3	Ⓐ	Ⓑ	Ⓒ
4	Ⓐ	Ⓑ	Ⓒ
5	Ⓐ	Ⓑ	Ⓒ
6	Ⓐ	Ⓑ	Ⓒ
7	Ⓐ	Ⓑ	Ⓒ
8	Ⓐ	Ⓑ	Ⓒ
9	Ⓐ	Ⓑ	Ⓒ
10	Ⓐ	Ⓑ	Ⓒ

2 Dictation 🎧

Listen and write the sentences you hear.

1. _____

_____

2. _____

_____

3. _____

_____

3 Conversation Check: Pair Work

Student A: Go to page 166.

Student B: Ask your partner questions
to complete this chart.

Student A: Go to page 166.

EXAMPLE: **B:** What did Jane have for an appetizer?
A: She didn't have an appetizer.
B: What did she have for a main dish?
A: She had fish stew.

Name	Appetizer	Main Dish	Dessert
Jane	XXXX	fish stew	
Sue	mushrooms	large salad	XXXXXX
Tim			
Tom	XXXXXX	a hamburger	a bowl of rice pudding

✔

How many questions did you ask your partner?	How many questions did you answer?
☐ 1　☐ 2　☐ 3　☐ 4　☐ 5　☐ 6	☐ 1　☐ 2　☐ 3　☐ 4　☐ 5　☐ 6

✔ LEARNING LOG

I know these words:

☐ appetizer	☐ dessert	☐ milk	☐ set the table
☐ bake	☐ eggs	☐ mix	☐ side order
☐ beverage	☐ fall off	☐ napkin	☐ slice
☐ boil	☐ fish	☐ oil	☐ soft drink
☐ booth	☐ flour	☐ peanuts	☐ soup
☐ bowl	☐ form a ball	☐ plate	☐ spill
☐ cereal	☐ fruit	☐ poultry	☐ sugar
☐ check	☐ fry	☐ pour	☐ take an order
☐ cheese	☐ heat	☐ red meat	☐ tray
☐ clear the table	☐ hostess	☐ roll	☐ trip over
☐ coffee	☐ ice cream	☐ salad	☐ vegetable
☐ counter	☐ main dish	☐ sandwich	☐ waiter
☐ cut up	☐ menu	☐ serve food	

I can ask:

☐ How much flour do you need?
☐ How many eggs do you want?
☐ Can you bring me a menu, please?
☐ What's your favorite dessert?
☐ How much was the tax?

I can say:

☐ I had fruit for breakfast yesterday.
☐ I'd like a small soup, please.
☐ I'd like a chicken sandwich.

I can write:

☐ a list of food
☐ a description of a restaurant
☐ a menu
☐ a recipe

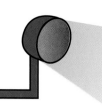

Spotlight: Writing

1 Read the restaurant review questionnaire. Answer the question below.

RESTAURANT REVIEW QUESTIONNAIRE

What's the name of the restaurant? _Tippy's Lunch_

What kind of food does it serve? _American_

How many people does it seat? _35_

	Yes	No
Is it clean?	☑	☐
Is it expensive?	☐	☑
Are children welcome?	☑	☐
Does it have good service?	☑	☐
Are the waiters friendly?	☑	☐
Does it have take out?	☑	☐
Is the food good?	☑	☐

Other: _not many healthy options_

FOCUS ON WRITING: Writing A Review

A good restaurant review uses descriptive language to help readers learn about the service, food, and price. Descriptive language includes adjectives that give interesting information. These adjectives help readers know if you like or dislike a restaurant.

EXAMPLES: **great** meatloaf
low prices
friendly waiters
unhealthy items

Do you want to go to Tippy's Lunch? Why or why not?

_____

_____

2 Read the restaurant review. Answer the questions.

Restaurant Reviews

Tippy's Lunch

Tippy's Lunch is a great place for a meal. It has great meatloaf, green beans, and mashed potatoes, all for low prices. It also has wonderful appetizers, burgers, chili, and soups. I really liked the friendly waiters and the fast service. Also, children are welcome. Tippy's is not the place to eat if you are on a diet. There are many unhealthy items on the menu. But if you want to eat great-tasting food, Tippy's is the place.

Service ★ ★ ★ ★
Food ★ ★ ★
Price $

1. Is Tippy's Lunch expensive?

_____

2. What food is good at Tippy's?

_____

_____

3. What is one problem with the food choices at Tippy's?

_____

3 Complete the questionnaire about a restaurant you know.

RESTAURANT REVIEW QUESTIONNAIRE

What's the name of the restaurant? _____

What kind of food does it serve? _____

How many people does it seat? _____

	Yes	No
Is it clean?	❑	❑
Is it expensive?	❑	❑
Are children welcome?	❑	❑
Does it have good service?	❑	❑
Are the waiters friendly?	❑	❑
Does it have take out?	❑	❑
Is the food good?	❑	❑

Other: _____

_____

---

4 Write a review about the restaurant. Use descriptive language to tell if you like or dislike the restaurant.

_____ (name of the restaurant)

_____

_____

_____

_____

_____

_____

Service

Food

Price

She's Juan's grandmother.

Manuel

THINGS TO DO

1 Learn New Words 🎧

Look at the pictures. Listen to the words. Then listen and repeat.

① grandparents ⑥ nephew ⑪ friend
② parents ⑦ niece ⑫ neighbors
③ aunt ⑧ fiancée ⑬ landlady
④ uncle ⑨ coworker
⑤ brother-in-law ⑩ boss

Which words are new to you? Circle them.

2 Ask Questions

Work with a partner. Ask about Juan's family and friends.

A: Who is Maria ?
B: She's Juan's grandmother .

 1 Tito 2 Paul 3 Lisa 4 💡

3 Interview

Work with a partner. Ask the questions below. Then tell the class about your partner.

1. How many aunts do you have? _____

2. Where do your parents live? _____

3. Do you know your neighbors? _____

4. Do you have a brother-in-law? What's his name?

_____

5. How many coworkers do you have? _____

★ ★

TRY THIS Make a diagram with information about your family. Use Juan's diagram as an example. Then tell a classmate about the people in your family.

★ ★

Richard   Lupe

Paul

Nick

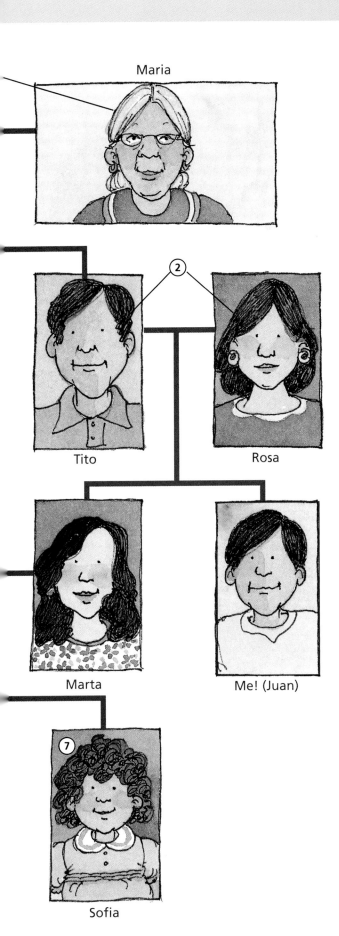

Maria

2

Tito

Rosa

Marta

Me! (Juan)

7

Sofia

Lisa

Tom

9

Mr. Li

10

11

Joe

12

Mrs. and Mr. Nath

Mrs. Chen

13

WINDOW ON GRAMMAR
Whose versus *Who's*

A Read the information below.

The pronunciation of *whose* and *who's* is the same. The meanings are very different. *Whose* asks about possession. *Who's* means *Who is*.

> EXAMPLES: **Whose** picture is it? **Whose** family is it?
>
> **Who's** in the picture? **Who's** Lisa?

B Write *Whose* or *Who's*. Then ask a classmate.

1. _____ Juan's fiancée?

2. _____ family is in the picture?

3. _____ book is this?

4. _____ parents live in the U.S.?

5. _____ going to study tonight?

101

2 LESSON

Who's dancing with Tito?

THINGS TO DO

1 Learn New Words 🎧

Look at the picture. Listen to the words. Then listen and repeat.

① bride
② groom
③ musicians
④ photographer

⑤ gifts
⑥ in a bad mood
⑦ kiss
⑧ make a toast

⑨ in a good mood
⑩ shake hands
⑪ hug
⑫ dance

Which words are new to you? Circle them.

2 Talk About the Picture

Write 5 things about the picture. Then share your ideas with the class.

EXAMPLE: The groom is standing next to the bride.

3 Practice the Conversation 🎧

Listen to the conversation. Then listen and repeat.

A: Who's dancing with Tito ?

B: That's the mother of the bride .

A: Do you know her name ?

B: Yes. It's Sylvia .

Practice the conversation with a partner. Use these ideas.

1 shaking hands with Maria	2 making a toast	3 talking to the photographer
the bride's grandfather	the groom's uncle	Juan's boss
his name	his first name	his name
Ted	Richard	Mr. Li

4 kissing Marta	5 looking at the gifts	6
one of her friends	the groom's niece	
his first name	her name	
Thomas	Sofia	

★ ★

TRY THIS Write 3–5 sentences about a wedding you attended. Answer these questions in your description: Whose wedding was it? Where was it? What did people do? Share your description with the class.

Sorry I'm late.

3 LESSON

THINGS TO DO

1 Learn New Words 🎧

Look at the pictures. Listen to the words. Then listen and repeat.

① ask for advice ④ apologize ⑦ criticize

② take care of ⑤ disagree ⑧ talk back

③ compliment ⑥ yell at

2 Ask Questions

Work with a partner. Take turns asking these questions.

DID YOU _____ YESTERDAY?	YES	NO	WHO?
ask anyone* for advice	☐	☐	_____
take care of anyone	☐	☐	_____
compliment anyone	☐	☐	_____
apologize to anyone	☐	☐	_____
disagree with anyone	☐	☐	_____
criticize anyone	☐	☐	_____

*Note: *anyone* means *any person.*

3 Practice the Conversation 🎧

Listen to the conversation. Then listen and repeat.

A: How was your day?

B: Not so good.

A: What happened?

B: My boss criticized me.

A: That's too bad. What did he say?

B: He said I was very disorganized .

Practice the conversation with a partner. Use these ideas.

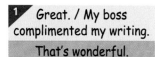

1 Great. / My boss complimented my writing.
That's wonderful.
it was very nice

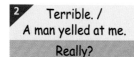

2 Terrible. / A man yelled at me.
Really?
I should slow down

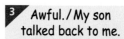

3 Awful. / My son talked back to me.
Really?
he didn't want to study

②

③

⑤

⑥

⑧

WINDOW ON GRAMMAR
Two-Word Verbs

A Read the information below.

Some verbs have two words. The meaning of the two words together is different from the meanings of the separate words.

> EXAMPLE: The verb *talk back* means *speak rudely*.

B Work with a partner. Read the sentences. Guess the meaning of each two-word verb.

1. Everyone **dressed up** for the wedding.

2. My father was 21 years old when he came to the U.S. He **grew up** in Mexico.

3. She **turned down** my invitation to dinner because she had to work.

105

⭐ **4**
LESSON

Family Traditions

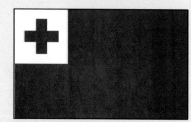

Tongan Flag

THINGS TO DO

1 Predict

Look at the pictures and the title of the reading on page 107. Read the sentences below. Check (✓) *I think so* or *I don't think so.*

	I THINK SO.	I DON'T THINK SO.
1. The Jets are family members.	☐	☐
2. The Jets are brothers and sisters.	☐	☐
3. The Jets are musicians.	☐	☐
4. The family is originally from the U.S.	☐	☐
5. This reading is about a group of doctors.	☐	☐
6. This reading is about real people.	☐	☐

Read the interview and check your predictions.

2 Read

Read the interview again and look for information to complete these sentences about LeRoy and The Jets.

1. LeRoy has _____ brothers and sisters.

2. He was born in _____.

3. His last name is _____.

4. LeRoy speaks English and _____.

5. Respecting your elders is a Tongan _____.

3 Interview and Write

Add 2 more questions about family to the list below. Then ask a classmate the questions. Write the interview for your classmates to read.

1. How many sisters and brothers do you have?

2. Are large families traditional in your culture?

3. Where did your brothers and sisters grow up?

4. _____

5. _____

> EXAMPLE: You: How many sisters and brothers do you have?
>
> Your Partner: I have 2 sisters and 2 brothers.

The Jets: All in the Family

To The Jets, music is **a family affair**. In fact, the eight members of this music group are all children of Mike and Vake Wolfgramm. The Wolfgramms are from Tonga, an island in the South Pacific. LeRoy is the oldest Jet.

Interviewer:	There are 15 children in your family. Are large families **traditional** in Tonga?
LeRoy:	Yes, they are.
Interviewer:	Did you all grow up in Tonga?
LeRoy:	Oh, no. I was the only one born there. But we were all **raised on** Tongan customs.
Interviewer:	What are some of the customs?
LeRoy:	Respecting your elders. Not talking back. Listening to your parents.
Interviewer:	With such a large family, how do you **deal with** the little problems that come up?
LeRoy:	We have family meetings. We talk about anything that **bothers** us. Like borrowing things without asking or taking too long in the bathroom.
Interviewer:	Do you speak Tongan?
LeRoy:	Yes, we speak Tongan at home. Usually, our parents speak to us in Tongan, and we answer in English.

a family affair: something the family does together

traditional: common, usual

raised on: taught

deal with: take care of

bother: make unhappy

WINDOW ON GRAMMAR
Nouns and Adjectives

 Read the sentences.

Noun Form

<u>Traditions</u> are important.

Buddhism is a <u>religion</u>.

Adjective Form

She wore a <u>traditional</u> dress.

He is a <u>religious</u> person.

 Complete the chart with the missing noun forms.

Noun	Adjective	Noun	Adjective
_____	problematic	_____	respectful
_____	customary	_____	elderly

LESSON 5

Do you really think so?

1 Practice the Conversation: Disagreeing Politely 🎧

Listen to the conversation. Then listen and repeat.

A: This is a great movie .

B: Do you really think so?

A: Yes, I love it. Don't you?

B: No, not really. I think it's kind of boring .

Practice the conversation with a partner.
Use these ideas.

1 terrific pizza / Yes, I think it's delicious.
too salty

2 wonderful house / Yes, I think it's beautiful.
kind of ugly inside

3 nice car / Yes, I think it's sporty.
kind of small

4

2 Practice the Conversation: Offering to Help 🎧

Listen to the conversation. Then listen and repeat.

A: Can I help you with the dishes ?

B: Thanks for offering but I'm all set .

A: Is there something else I can do ?

B: No, but thanks.

Practice the conversation with a partner.
Use these ideas.

1 carry that box
I can get it
I can carry

2 write the invitations
I'm almost finished
I can do for the wedding

3 clear the table
I can do it
I can help you with

4

3 Practice the Conversation: Accepting Help 🎧

Listen to the conversation. Then listen and repeat.

A: Would you like me to mail this letter ?

B: Thank you. That would be great .

A: Is there anything else I can do?

B: No, but thanks for offering.

Practice the conversation with a partner.
Use these ideas.

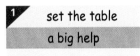

1	set the table
	a big help

Can I do anything else?

2	help in the kitchen
	very helpful

Would you like me to clear the table, too?

3	call Ms. Smith
	nice

Is there something else I can do?

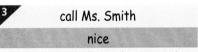

4

WINDOW ON PRONUNCIATION 🎧
Suffixes and Syllable Stress

 A Listen to the words. Then listen and repeat.

Base word	+ suffix		Base word	+ suffix
1. apology	apologize		6. invite	invitation
2. recreation	recreational		7. marry	marital
3. critic	criticize		8. music	musician
4. drama	dramatic		9. problem	problematic
5. identify	identification		10. tradition	traditional

Underline the syllable that receives the most stress.

 B Write the words in the correct place in the chart.

-ic suffix	*-ize* suffix	*-al* suffix	*-ion/-ian* suffix
dramatic			

Which suffixes change the stress? _____

109

UNIT 7: Relationships

Invitations, Presents, and Packages

1 Learn New Words 🎧

Listen to the words for items you can mail. Then listen and repeat.

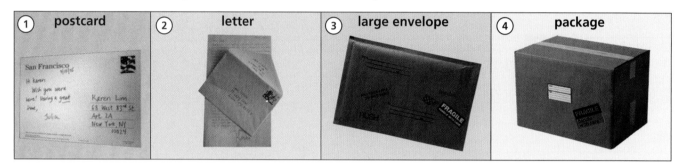

| ① postcard | ② letter | ③ large envelope | ④ package |

2 Read and Check *True* or *False*

Look at the chart. Read the questions below about U.S. postal services. Check (✓) *True* or *False*.

Service	Items You Can Mail	Cost	Speed
Express Mail	letter large envelope package (70 lbs. or less)	$$$ based on weight	1–2 days guaranteed
Priority Mail	large envelope package (70 lbs. or less)	$$ based on weight and distance if over 1 pound	1–3 days
First-Class Mail	postcard letter large envelope package (13 oz. or less)	$ based on weight	1–3 days
Parcel Post	package (70 lbs. or less)	$ based on weight and distance	2–9 days

1. Parcel post is the slowest way to send a package.   ☐ True   ☐ False
2. First-class mail is the most expensive way to send a letter.   ☐ True   ☐ False
3. Express mail is the fastest way to send a letter.   ☐ True   ☐ False
4. You can send a letter by parcel post.   ☐ True   ☐ False

3 Evaluate

Choose the best postal service for each situation below.

Situation #1	Situation #2	Situation #3
David is in New York. He has to send a package to his boss in California. She is making a presentation there in two days. It is important that the package is on time. The cost is not important.	Marta is mailing her brother's wedding invitations. Her brother is getting married in two months. The invitations are in small envelopes. She wants the invitations to arrive in a few days.	Julie is sending two packages. One is a wedding present for a friend. The other is a graduation present for her cousin. She has lots of time. Both packages are over 2 pounds.
Best Way to Mail It	Best Way to Mail Them	Best Way to Mail Them
Reason	Reason	Reason

WINDOW ON MATH
Ounces and Pounds

16 ounces (oz.) = 1 pound (lb.)

 Answer these questions.

1. Your package weighs 5 pounds. How many ounces does it weigh?

2. You have to send a package that weighs 18 oz. Which U.S. postal services can you use?

3. Your package weighs 48 oz. If it costs $1.50 per lb. to mail it, how much does it cost?

4. The maximum weight for a package is 70 lbs. How many ounces is that?

LESSON 7

What do you know?

1 Listening Review 🎧

Listen to the conversations. Choose the best answer. Use the Answer Sheet.

1. A. She complimented him.
   B. She apologized to him.
   C. She criticized him.

2. A. She offered to help.
   B. He offered to help.
   C. He asked her to help.

3. A. He yelled at her.
   B. He apologized to her.
   C. He criticized her.

4. A. She asked him for advice.
   B. She talked back to him.
   C. She yelled at him.

5. A. He complimented her.
   B. She complimented him.
   C. He disagreed with her.

ANSWER SHEET

1	Ⓐ	Ⓑ	Ⓒ
2	Ⓐ	Ⓑ	Ⓒ
3	Ⓐ	Ⓑ	Ⓒ
4	Ⓐ	Ⓑ	Ⓒ
5	Ⓐ	Ⓑ	Ⓒ

2 Listen and Write 🎧

Who are the people in the picture? Listen first. Then complete the sentences. Then listen again and check your answers.

1. Gino is Ben's _____.

2. Don is Ben's _____.

3. Tina is Ben's _____.

4. Joe is Ben's _____.

5. Ann is Ben's _____.

3 Conversation Check: Pair Work

Student A: Go to page 167.

Student B: Ask your partner questions to complete this chart.

EXAMPLE: **B:** Who is John?
A: He's Rick's uncle.
B: What's his occupation?

Name	John	Lana	Sam	Gino
Relationship to Rick	*Rick's uncle*	Rick's niece		Rick's coworker
Occupation				

✔

How many questions did you ask your partner?	How many questions did you answer?
☐ 1 ☐ 2 ☐ 3 ☐ 4	☐ 1 ☐ 2 ☐ 3 ☐ 4

✔ LEARNING LOG

I know these words:

- ☐ apologize
- ☐ ask for advice
- ☐ aunt
- ☐ boss
- ☐ bother
- ☐ bride
- ☐ brother-in-law
- ☐ compliment
- ☐ coworker
- ☐ criticize
- ☐ custom
- ☐ customary

- ☐ dance
- ☐ deal with
- ☐ disagree
- ☐ dress up
- ☐ elder
- ☐ elderly
- ☐ employer
- ☐ family affair
- ☐ fiancée
- ☐ friend
- ☐ gifts
- ☐ grandparents

- ☐ groom
- ☐ grow up
- ☐ hug
- ☐ in a bad mood
- ☐ in a good mood
- ☐ invitation
- ☐ kiss
- ☐ landlady
- ☐ make a toast
- ☐ musicians
- ☐ neighbors
- ☐ nephew

- ☐ niece
- ☐ package
- ☐ parents
- ☐ photographer
- ☐ postcard
- ☐ problem
- ☐ problematic
- ☐ raised on
- ☐ religion
- ☐ religious
- ☐ respect
- ☐ respectful

- ☐ shake hands
- ☐ take care of
- ☐ talk back
- ☐ tradition
- ☐ traditional
- ☐ turn down
- ☐ uncle
- ☐ yell at

I can ask:

- ☐ Where do your grandparents live?
- ☐ What are your parents' first names?
- ☐ Whose family is it?
- ☐ Who's in the picture?
- ☐ Who's dancing with . . . ?
- ☐ Do you know her name?
- ☐ What did he say?
- ☐ How was your day?
- ☐ Can I help with the dishes?
- ☐ Is there anything else I can do?

I can say:

- ☐ The groom is standing next to the bride.
- ☐ My boss criticized me.
- ☐ The verb "talk back" means "speak rudely."
- ☐ Thanks for offering but I'm all set.

I can write:

- ☐ information in a family diagram
- ☐ a description of a wedding
- ☐ interview questions and answers

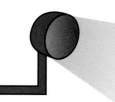

Spotlight: Grammar

TWO-WORD VERBS

- Some verbs have two words. The meaning of the two words together is different from the meanings of the separate words.

   EXAMPLES: Children **grow up**. (grow up = become adults)
   The waiter **waited on** us right away. (waited on = took our food order)
   She **called up** all her friends. (called up = telephoned)

- You can separate many two-word verbs with a noun or object pronoun.

   EXAMPLES: She **called** <u>her sister</u> **up**. She **called** <u>her</u> **up**.

- A noun can go between or after the two words.   • An object pronoun can only go between the two words.
   EXAMPLES: He **looked up** <u>the word</u>.   EXAMPLE: He **looked** <u>it</u> **up**.
   He **looked** <u>the word</u> **up**.

---

1 Complete each conversation. Use an object pronoun in place of the underlined noun.

1. A: Did you fill out <u>the application form</u>?

   B: Yes, I did. I _____ *filled it out* _____ this morning.

2. A: Did you take out <u>the trash</u>?

   B: Yes, I did. I _____ yesterday.

3. A: Did your teacher hand out <u>the examinations</u>?

   B: Yes, she did. She _____ yesterday.

4. A: Was it difficult to find out <u>his mailing address</u>?

   B: No, it was easy to _____ .

5. A: Did you look up <u>Laura</u> in the telephone book?

   B: Yes, I _____ and I called last week.

TIP
Object Pronouns

me	you
him	us
her	them
it	

2 Rewrite each sentence. Use an object pronoun.

1. He looked up her telephone number in the telephone book.

   He looked it up in the telephone book.
   _____

2. He checked out the book from the library.

   _____

3. She bought a new coat and put on the new coat.

   _____

4. He found her telephone number and wrote down her telephone number.

   _____

COUNT NOUNS AND NONCOUNT NOUNS

Count Nouns	Noncount Nouns

• Count nouns have a singular and a plural form.
 	
  EXAMPLES: student—students
     brother—brothers
	• Noncount nouns are always singular.
	
	  EXAMPLES: money furniture
	     music coffee

• You can use *a* or *an* with the singular form of count nouns.
 	
  EXAMPLES: a brother, an aunt, a family
	• You don't use *a* or *an* with noncount nouns.
	
	  EXAMPLES: I like music.
	     I love coffee.

• You can use *many, a lot of, a few,* and *any* with the plural form of count nouns.
 	
  EXAMPLE: I have many aunts, a lot of cousins, and a few nieces. I don't have any nephews.
	• You can use *much, a lot of, a little,* and *any* with noncount nouns.
	
	  EXAMPLE: I drank too much coffee. I ate a lot of fruit and a little meat. I didn't eat any bread.
	
	• We often use quantity words with noncount nouns.
	
	  EXAMPLE: I drank a cup of coffee. I bought a loaf of bread.

3 Read the sentences. Is the **boldfaced** word a count noun or a noncount noun? Write *C* (count noun) or *NC* (noncount noun) next to each question.

1. Do you have any **sisters**? _C_
2. Do you have any **furniture**? _____
3. Do you have a lot of **work**? _____
4. Do you have a lot of **friends**? _____
5. Do you have a few **stamps**? _____
6. Do you have a little **milk**? _____
7. Do you have some **sugar**? _____

8. Do you have some **envelopes**? _____
9. Do you have a **telephone** at home? _____
10. Do you have **electricity** at home? _____
11. Do you have **chairs** at home? _____
12. How much **money** did it cost? _____
13. How many **packages** did you send? _____
14. Do you want a **bowl** of cereal? _____

4 Complete the sentences. Choose the correct word in parentheses.

1. Did you buy many _____? (books / furniture)
2. He bought _____ stamps at the post office. (a few / a little)
3. She is putting _____ milk in her coffee. (a few / a little)
4. A lot of chairs _____ empty. (is / are)
5. Some clothing _____ on sale this week. (is / are)
6. How _____ tea do you want? (many / much)
7. How _____ students are in your class? (many / much)
8. Do you want _____ cup of coffee? (a / some)

LESSON 1

Muscles, Bones, and Joints

THINGS TO DO

1 Learn New Words 🎧

Look at the pictures. Listen to the words. Then listen and repeat.

① brain   ④ waist   ⑦ bone   ⑩ heart
② tooth*   ⑤ hip   ⑧ skin   ⑪ lungs
③ muscle   ⑥ joint   ⑨ blood   ⑫ back

*Note: the plural of *tooth* is *teeth.*

Write the new words on the lines.

2 Write

Complete the chart with parts of the body for each category below. Then compare lists with a partner.

I have muscles in my _____.	I have bones in my _____.	My _____ is a joint.
1. _____arm_____	1. _____finger_____	1. _____shoulder_____
2. _____	2. _____	2. _____
3. _____	3. _____	3. _____
4. _____	4. _____	
5. _____	5. _____	

3 Check Your Answers

Read the statements. Check (✓) *True, False,* or *I don't know.* Then correct the false statements.

	True	False	I don't know
1. You breathe with your lungs.	☐	☐	☐
2. Your elbow is between your shoulder and wrist.	☐	☐	☐
3. An ankle is a joint.	☐	☐	☐
4. You have skin on your teeth.	☐	☐	☐
5. Your heart moves your blood around.	☐	☐	☐
6. You have more bones than teeth.	☐	☐	☐
7. Two bones meet at a joint.	☐	☐	☐
8. Your brain is a muscle.	☐	☐	☐

★ ★ ★ ★ ★ ★ ★ ★ ★ ★ ★ ★ ★ ★
TRY THIS Work with a partner. Take turns giving instructions, using words for different body parts.

EXAMPLES:
Point to your left ear.
Point to your right ankle.
★ ★ ★ ★ ★ ★ ★ ★ ★ ★ ★ ★ ★ ★

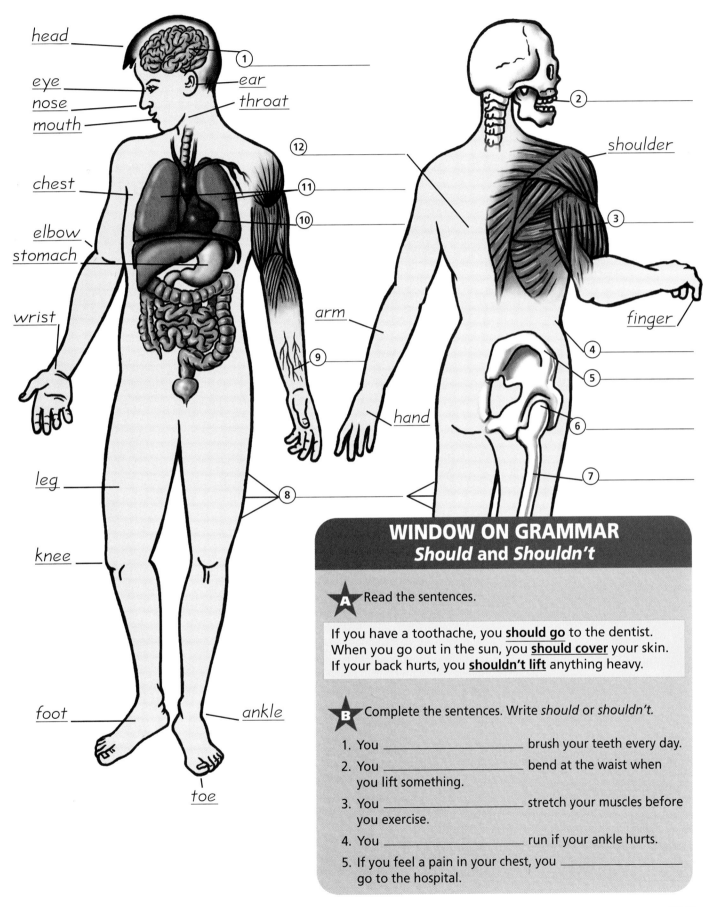

head
eye
nose
mouth
ear
throat
chest
elbow
stomach
wrist
leg
knee
foot
toe
ankle
shoulder
arm
finger
hand

1
2
3
4
5
6
7
8
9
10
11
12

WINDOW ON GRAMMAR
Should and *Shouldn't*

A Read the sentences.

If you have a toothache, you **should go** to the dentist.
When you go out in the sun, you **should cover** your skin.
If your back hurts, you **shouldn't lift** anything heavy.

B Complete the sentences. Write *should* or *shouldn't*.

1. You _____ brush your teeth every day.
2. You _____ bend at the waist when you lift something.
3. You _____ stretch your muscles before you exercise.
4. You _____ run if your ankle hurts.
5. If you feel a pain in your chest, you _____ go to the hospital.

117

Maybe you should see a doctor.

Injuries

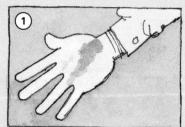

THINGS TO DO

1 Learn New Words 🎧

Look at the pictures. Listen to the words. Then listen and repeat.

- ① burn
- ② cut
- ③ fracture
- ④ sprain
- ⑤ bruise
- ⑥ shock
- ⑦ rash
- ⑧ fever
- ⑨ cold
- ⑩ flu
- ⑪ infection
- ⑫ feel dizzy
- ⑬ blister
- ⑭ feel nauseous
- ⑮ bleed

Which words are new to you? Circle them.

2 Practice the Conversation 🎧

Listen to the conversation. Then listen and repeat.

A: Is your rash getting any better?

B: No, I don't think so.

A: Maybe you should see a doctor .

B: Maybe you're right.

Practice the conversation with a partner. Ask about these things.

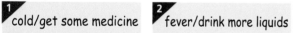
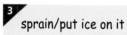

| 1 cold/get some medicine | 2 fever/drink more liquids | 3 sprain/put ice on it |
| 4 head cold/lie down | 5 cut/go to the doctor | 6 💡 |

3 Write

Complete the sentences below. Then compare ideas with the class.

1. You should go to the doctor if ___you have a high fever___.
2. You should rest if _____.
3. You should stay off your feet if _____.
4. You should stay at home if _____.
5. You should _____ if you have a cold.

★ ★

TRY THIS Use the Internet or your local phone book to find information about health services in your area. Write down the address and phone number of a clinic and a hospital near you.

★ ★

Symptoms and Illnesses

WINDOW ON GRAMMAR
Might and *Will*

A Read the sentences.

> If you cut your hand, it **will** bleed.
> If you touch poison ivy, you **might** get a rash.
> If you burn your hand, you **might** get a blister.

B Match the causes and effects.

Causes	Effects
1. If you break your leg,	you won't be able to write.
2. If you smoke,	you might have the flu.
3. If you feel nauseous,	you might have a stomach flu.
4. If you feel dizzy,	you won't be able to walk.
5. If you hurt your hand,	you will hurt your lungs.

3
LESSON

Did you go to the emergency room?

THINGS TO DO

1 Learn New Words 🎧

Look at the picture. Listen to the words. Then listen and repeat.

1. emergency room
2. examining room
3. x-ray
4. radiology
5. stitches
6. sling
7. ice pack
8. admissions desk
9. splint
10. wheelchair
11. waiting room
12. crutches
13. cast
14. bandage

Which words are new to you? Circle them.

2 Talk About the Picture

Write 5 questions about the picture. Then ask your classmates your questions.

> EXAMPLES: What is wrong with Lupe's child?
> Who's using crutches?

3 Practice the Conversation 🎧

Listen to the conversation. Then listen and repeat.

A: What happened to your leg ?

B: I sprained my knee .

A: Did you have to go to the emergency room?

B: Yes, a friend took me there.

A: Did they take an x-ray ?

B: Yes, and then they put this splint on my knee .

Practice the conversation with a partner. Use these ideas.

1	hand
	cut it
	stitch it up
	put this bandage on it

2	leg
	broke it
	put you in a wheelchair
	put this cast on

3	elbow
	sprained it
	put ice on it
	put this sling on it

4	back
	bruised it
	take an x-ray
	gave me this ice pack

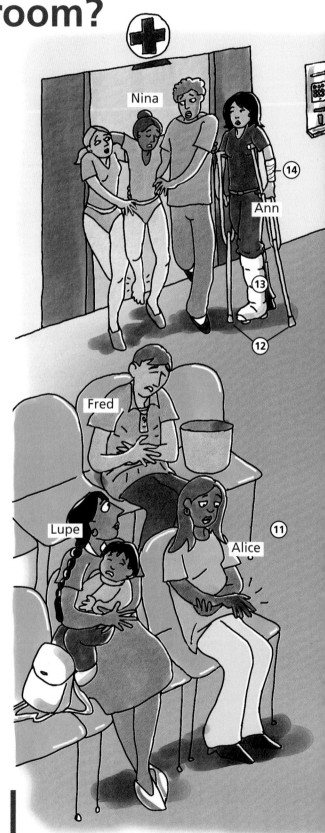

Nina

Ann

⑭

⑬

⑫

Fred

Lupe

Alice

⑪

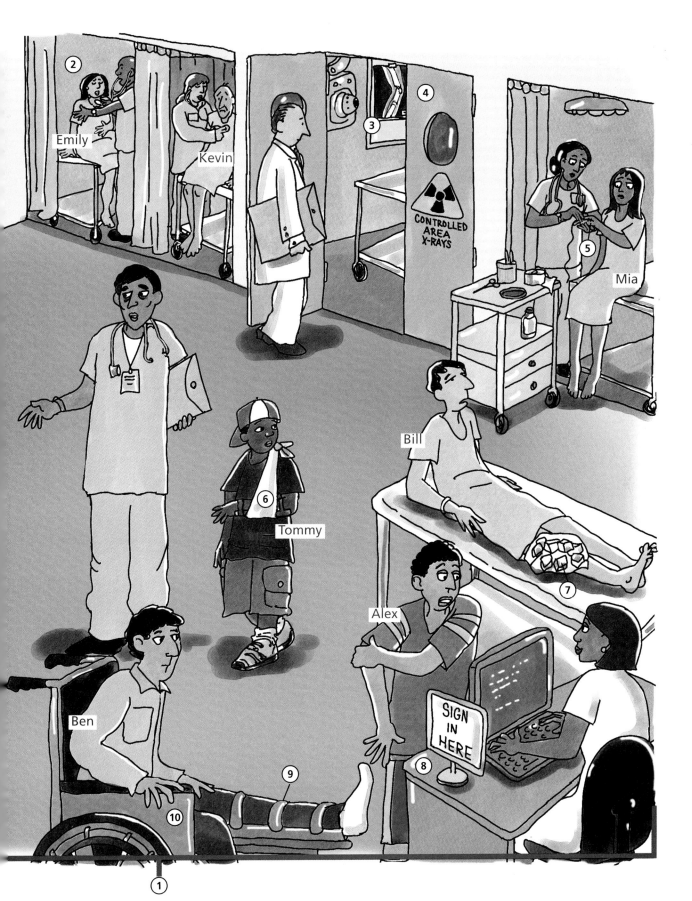

4
LESSON

Medicine Labels

THINGS TO DO

1 Learn New Words 🎧

Look at the medicine labels. Listen to the words. Then listen and repeat.

① **tablet**　② **teaspoon**　③ **cream**　④ **OTC**　⑤ **capsule**

2 Read and Take Notes

Read the labels and complete the chart below.

Name of medicine	Form	How much?	How often?
A. acetaminophen	tablet		every 46 hours
B.	liquid		
C. hydrocortisone		-----	
D.		1	

OTC = over the counter, or without a prescription

3 Check *True* or *False*

Read the statements. Check (✓) *True* or *False*. Then correct the false statements.

	True	False
1. Children older than six can take acetaminophen.	☐	☐
2. You can swallow hydrocortisone cream.	☐	☐
3. Children under age 12 can take Max-Relief.	☐	☐
4. Ampicillin and Max-Relief are OTC.	☐	☐
5. Dr. Dickinson prescribed the hydrocortisone.	☐	☐
6. The ampicillin is for Claire Donnalley.	☐	☐
7. You can use the ampicillin in 2008.	☐	☐
8. Acetaminophen is a prescription medicine.	☐	☐

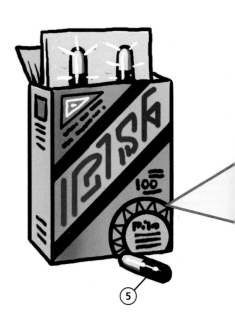

4 Write

Make a chart like this. Write the health problem or symptom next to the medicine.

NAME OF MEDICINE	USE THE MEDICINE FOR THESE PROBLEMS
Acetaminophen	headache, backache, …
Max-Relief	
Hydrocortisone	

A **Acetaminophen**

100 tablets 325 mg

For pain due to:

headache   toothache

backache   a cold

muscle aches

Directions: Do not take more than directed. Adults and children 12 years or older: take 2 tablets every 4 to 6 hours.

Keep out of reach of children.

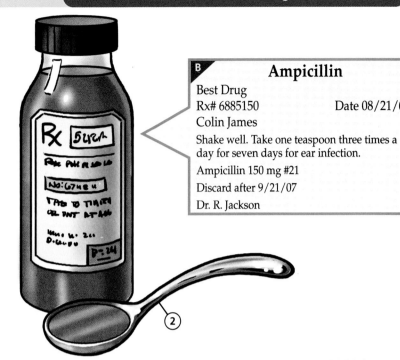

B **Ampicillin**

Best Drug

Rx# 6885150   Date 08/21/07

Colin James

Shake well. Take one teaspoon three times a day for seven days for ear infection.

Ampicillin 150 mg #21

Discard after 9/21/07

Dr. R. Jackson

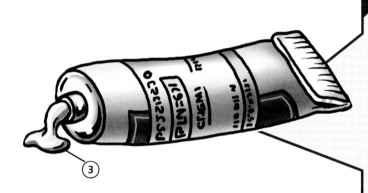

C **Hydrocortisone cream**

Drug Fair

RX# 74432   Date 12/03/06

Claire Donnalley

Wash skin. Apply to affected area 3 to 4 times a day to relieve pain, swelling, and itching due to rashes.

Pr. by A. Dickinson, MD

Warnings: For external use only. Do not swallow. Do not use near eyes. KEEP THIS AND ALL DRUGS OUT OF THE REACH OF CHILDREN. If swallowed, call a Poison Control Center immediately.

D **Max-Relief Cold and Flu** ④

The strongest medicine available without a prescription. For fever, headache, body aches, runny nose, and sneezing associated with a cold or flu.

12 capsules   Take 1 capsule every 12 hours.

Warnings:
  Ask a doctor before use if you have breathing problems, lung, or heart disease.
  Do not give to children under 12 years of age.

WINDOW ON MATH
Ounces, Tablespoons, and Teaspoons

1 tablespoon (tbsp.) = 3 teaspoons (tsp.)

2 tablespoons (tbsp.) = 1 fluid ounce (fl. oz.)

A Complete the sentences.

1. 2 tbsp. = _____ tsp.

2. 1 tbsp. = _____ fl. oz.

3. 6 tsp. = _____ fl. oz.

4. 1.5 tsp. = _____ tbsp.

5. ½ fl. oz. = _____ tsp.

LESSON 5

What happened?

1 Practice the Conversation: Describing an Illness 🎧

Listen to the conversation. Then listen and repeat.

A: I'd like to make an appointment as soon as possible.

B: What's the problem?

A: I have a high fever.

B: Do your joints hurt?

A: Yes.

B: I have an opening this afternoon.

A: Great. I'll take it.

Practice the conversation with a partner.
Use these items.

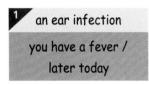

1	an ear infection
	you have a fever / later today

2	a toothache
	you have any bleeding / tomorrow morning

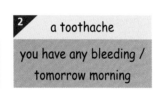

3	the flu
	you feel nauseous / this morning

4

2 Practice the Conversation: Describing an Injury 🎧

Listen to the conversation. Then listen and repeat.

A: What happened?

B: I got injured in a soccer game.

A: What hurts?

B: My elbow.

A: You may have a sprain. Let's take a look.

Practice the conversation with a partner.
Use these items.

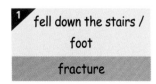

1	fell down the stairs / foot
	fracture

2	had an accident at work / hip
	bruise

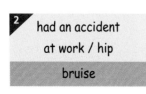

3	slipped on some ice / ankle
	sprain

4

3 Practice the Conversation: Following Instructions 🎧

Listen to the conversation. Then listen and repeat.

A: Use this sling until the next appointment.
   Here's a prescription for some pain medication.
B: How often do I take it?
A: Take 1 tablet 2 times a day . Don't take more
   than that.
B: Can I play soccer ?
A: No. Not until I see you again.

Practice the conversation with a partner.
Use these items.

| 1 | these crutches / 2 tablets 3 times a day |
| drive my car |

| 2 | this ice pack as needed / 2 capsules 4 times a day |
| go back to work |

| 3 | this splint / 1 tablet 4 times a day |
| exercise |

| 4 |

WINDOW ON PRONUNCIATION 🎧
Can Versus Can't

A Listen to the sentences. Then listen and repeat.

1. Can I play soccer?
2. Can't I play soccer?
3. Children can take some medicines.
4. Children can't take aspirin.
5. You can fill this prescription at the drugstore.
6. You can't take the medicine after the expiration date.

B Listen to the sentences. Underline the word you hear.

1. He can / <u>can't</u> come to school today.

2. She can / can't go back to work.

3. They can / can't hear the teacher.

4. I can / can't exercise today.

C Work with a partner. Take turns reading the sentences
in Activity B. Respond with *Oh, good.* or *That's too bad.*

EXAMPLE: A: He can come to school today.
          B: Oh, good.

Accident Reports

1 Answer the Questions

Read the accident report below. Answer the questions.

1. What is the injured person's name?

   _____

2. What happened?

   _____

3. When did the accident happen?

   _____

4. What body part did he injure?

   _____

5. What kind of injury was it?

   _____

EMPLOYEE ACCIDENT REPORT

Name of employee: _Daniel Young_   SSN: _563-55-4321_

Address: _1952 Glenbrook Road, Fairfax_   D.O.B.: _10/27/64_

Workplace: _Fairfax Hospital_   Position: _Nursing Assistant_

Normal working hours: _7-3_   Part time: _____   Full time: _X_

Date of accident: _6/15/05_   Time of accident: _12:15 p.m._

How did the accident happen? _Mr. Young slipped on the wet floor._

Part of the Body Injured			Type of Injury	
☐ ankle	☐ elbow	☐ head	☒ bruise	☐ fracture
☐ arm	☐ finger	☐ knee	☐ burn	☐ sprain
☒ back	☐ foot	☐ leg	☐ cut	
☐ chest	☐ hand	☐ shoulder		

Supervisor's name: _Laura Hill_

Employee's signature: _Daniel Young_

2 Write

Use the information below to complete the accident report for Robert Garza.

CALIFORNIA
DRIVER LICENSE
EXPIRES: 04-19-07   7805067644   CLASS: 2

ROBERT MANUEL GARZA
1521 MARKET STREET ⑨
SAN FRANCISCO, CA
94821

⑪
DOB: 03-02-75

HAIR: BRN   EYES: BRN
HT: 5'10"   WT: 160 LBS
⑫   ⑬

Robert Garza

time of accident

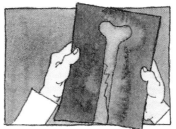

Robert's arm

SAN FRANCISCO GENERAL HOSPITAL

Robert Garza
Nursing Assistant

EMPLOYEE ACCIDENT REPORT

Name of employee: Robert Garza   **SSN:** 028-55-1113

Address: _____ **D.O.B.:** _____

Workplace: _____ **Position:** _____

Normal working hours: 3–11   **Part time:** _____ **Full time:** X

Date of accident: _____ **Time of accident:** _____
(use today's date)

How did the accident happen? Mr. Garza fell down the stairs.

Part of the Body Injured			Type of Injury	
☐ ankle	☐ elbow	☐ head	☐ bruise	☐ fracture
☐ arm	☐ finger	☐ knee	☐ burn	☐ sprain
☐ back	☐ foot	☐ leg	☐ cut	
☐ chest	☐ hand	☐ shoulder		

Supervisor's name: Ellen Martin

Employee's signature: *Robert Garza*

LESSON 7

What do you know?

1 Listening Review 🎧

Listen and choose the best answer. Use the Answer Sheet.

1. A. You can take eight tablets a day.
   B. You can take six tablets a day.
   C. You can take two capsules two times a day.

2. A. You hurt your arm.
   B. You hurt your leg.
   C. You hurt your hip.

3. A. Give it to children.
   B. Put it in a safe place, away from children.
   C. Ask your doctor before you give it to children.

4. A. I have a problem with my back.
   B. I have a problem with my wrist.
   C. I have a problem with my stomach.

5. A. That's terrible.
   B. Playing soccer.
   C. I have a doctor's appointment.

6. A. My ankle.
   B. My ear.
   C. My stomach.

7. A. That's good news.
   B. That's too bad.
   C. Yes, please.

8. A. I have the flu.
   B. We won our game.
   C. No, thanks.

9. A. Playing soccer.
   B. Yes, I sprained it.
   C. No, I sprained it.

10. A. She gave me crutches.
    B. I have the flu.
    C. I fractured it.

ANSWER SHEET			
1	A	B	C
2	A	B	C
3	A	B	C
4	A	B	C
5	A	B	C
6	A	B	C
7	A	B	C
8	A	B	C
9	A	B	C
10	A	B	C

2 Dictation 🎧

Listen and write the sentences you hear.

1. _____

2. _____

3. _____

3 Conversation Check: Pair Work

Student A: Go to page 167.

Student B: Ask your partner questions to complete this chart.

EXAMPLE: **B:** What's the matter with Chris?
A: He has a sprained ankle.
B: What did the doctor give him?

Name	What's the matter with him/her?	What did the doctor give him/her?
1. Chris	*He has a sprained ankle.*	
2. Mary		
3. Cynthia		
4. Alex		

✔

How many questions did you ask your partner?	How many questions did you answer?
☐ 1 ☐ 2 ☐ 3 ☐ 4	☐ 1 ☐ 2 ☐ 3 ☐ 4

✔ LEARNING LOG

I know these words:

☐ admissions desk	☐ capsule	☐ fever	☐ muscle	☐ stitches
☐ back	☐ cast	☐ flu	☐ OTC	☐ tablet
☐ bandage	☐ cold	☐ fracture	☐ radiology	☐ teaspoon
☐ bleed	☐ cream	☐ heart	☐ rash	☐ teeth
☐ blister	☐ crutches	☐ hip	☐ shock	☐ tooth
☐ blood	☐ cut	☐ ice pack	☐ skin	☐ waist
☐ bone	☐ emergency room	☐ infection	☐ sling	☐ waiting room
☐ brain	☐ examining room	☐ joint	☐ splint	☐ wheelchair
☐ bruise	☐ feel dizzy	☐ lungs	☐ sprain	☐ x-ray
☐ burn	☐ feel nauseous			

I can ask:

☐ Is your rash getting any better?
☐ What happened to your leg?
☐ What's wrong with Lupe's child?
☐ Did you have to go to the emergency room?
☐ How often do I take it?

I can say:

☐ You should go to the dentist.
☐ Maybe you should see a doctor.
☐ I sprained my knee.
☐ I'd like to make an appointment.

I can write:

☐ a description of an injury
☐ information on an accident report

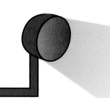

Spotlight: Writing

1 Read the story. Under each picture below write the cause and the effect.

How I Got This Scar

Do you see this scar on my hand? Let me tell you how it happened. When I was 23, I had a car accident. Because it was raining, my car hit a tree. I cut my face and I broke three bones in my foot. I also broke a bone in my hand. The doctors stitched the cut on my face. They put a cast on my foot. The bone in my hand was fractured, so I needed surgery. The doctors put a pin in the bone of my hand. The pin held the bone together so it could heal. One day, a doctor took the pin out. Because of the surgery, I now have this scar.

FOCUS ON WRITING: Cause and Effect

When we write a story, we often use cause and effect sentences to tell what happened. A cause is the reason for something. An effect is the result.

EXAMPLES:

(cause)   (effect)
Because it was raining, my car hit a tree.

(cause)
The bone in my hand was fractured,

(effect)
so I needed surgery.

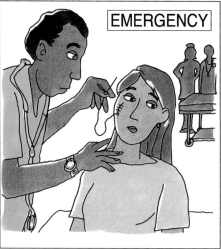

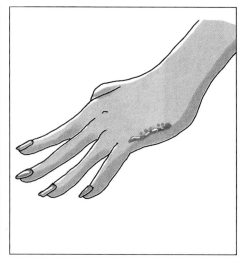

Cause: _____ _rain_ _____

Effect: _____

Cause: _____

Effect: _____ _stitches_ _____

Cause: _____

Effect: _____

2 Answer the questions about you.

1. Where do you have a scar? _____

2. What happened? _____

3. Why did it happen? _____

4. When did it happen? _____

3 Write a story about your scar. Use your answers in Activity 2. Use cause and effect sentences to tell what happened.

HOW I GOT THIS SCAR

_____

_____

_____

_____

_____

_____

_____

_____

_____

_____

_____

_____

_____

_____

_____

1 LESSON

Did I unplug the coffeepot?

THINGS TO DO

1 Learn New Words 🎧

Look at the pictures. Listen to the words. Then listen and repeat.

① shut off   ⑤ turn off   ⑧ lock
② plug in   ⑥ put back   ⑨ unlock
③ take out   ⑦ turn down   ⑩ unplug
④ turn on

2 Write

Make a chart like this. Write 3 things you see in each room.

BEDROOM	KITCHEN	LIVING ROOM
a lamp	a refrigerator	

Now use the pictures to tell what Mr. Sanchez did this morning. See page 174 for past tense of irregular verbs.

EXAMPLE: Mr. Sanchez shut off the alarm clock.

3 Practice the Conversation 🎧

Listen to the conversation. Then listen and repeat

A: Could you unplug the heater for me?

B: Sure. Where is it ?

A: It's in the bedroom .

B: Okay. I'll do it right away.

Practice the conversation with a partner. Use these ideas.

1 turn down the heat	2 plug in the fan	3 lock the front door	4
the thermostat	it	the key	
in the dining room	in the living room	on the table	

①

⑤

⑨

WINDOW ON GRAMMAR
Commands and Requests

A Read the sentences.

COMMANDS:	Turn down the radio.
	Don't lock the door.
REQUESTS:	Could you please turn down the radio?
	Would you please not lock the door?

B Rewrite each command as a polite request.

1. Shut off the TV now. _____

2. Turn off the lights. _____

3. Don't turn off the radio. _____

   _____

4. Don't put the milk away. _____

   _____

133

2 LESSON

The sink's leaking.

① **Things that leak**

THINGS TO DO

1 Learn New Words 🎧

Look at the pictures. Listen to the words. Then listen and repeat.

① leak
② faucet
③ pipe
④ roof
⑤ overheat
⑥ space heater

⑦ clothes dryer
⑧ hair dryer
⑨ get plugged up
⑩ sink
⑪ toilet
⑫ bathtub

⑬ get stuck
⑭ key
⑮ elevator
⑯ sliding door

⑤ **Things that overheat**

2 Practice the Conversation 🎧

Listen to the telephone conversation. Then listen and repeat.

A: Hi. This is your tenant in apartment 101.

B: Hi. What can I do for you?

A: Could you please take a look at my refrigerator ?

B: Is the door stuck again?

A: No. This time it's leaking .

B: Okay. I'll be over as soon as I can.

⑨ **Things that get plugged up**

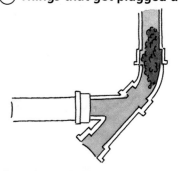

Practice the conversation with a partner. Use these ideas.

1 dryer	**2** sliding door	**3** bathroom sink	**4**
Is it overheating	Is it stuck	Is it leaking	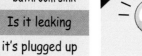
the door is stuck	I can't lock it	it's plugged up	

3 Write

Choose a problem from Activity 2. Complete the form below.

⑬ **Things that get stuck**

MAINTENANCE REQUEST FORM

Date:	
Time:	
Name:	
Problem:	
Signature:	

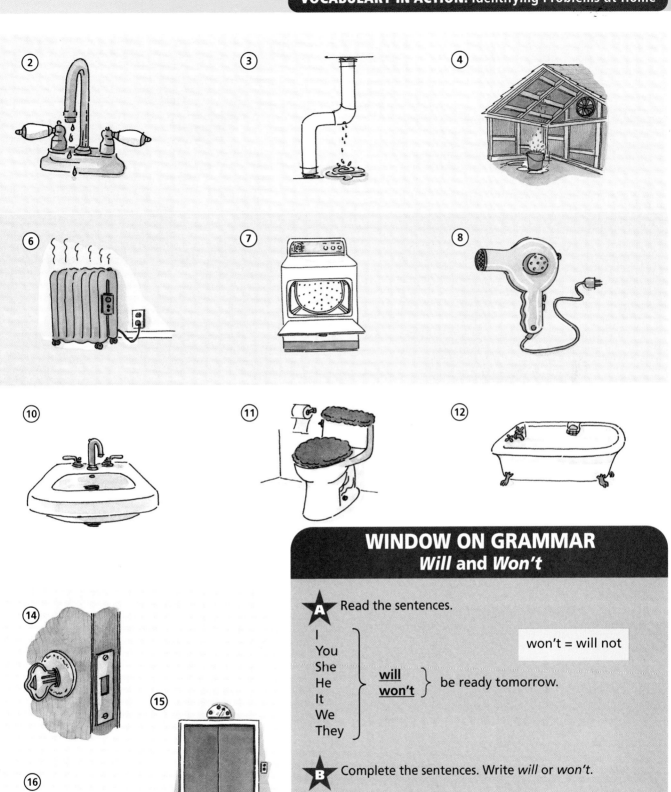

WINDOW ON GRAMMAR
Will and *Won't*

A Read the sentences.

I		
You		
She		
He	**will**	be ready tomorrow.
It	**won't**	
We		
They		

won't = will not

B Complete the sentences. Write *will* or *won't*.

1. If the pipe breaks it _____ leak.

2. If the dryer is overheating, I _____ turn it up.

3. If the faucet is leaking, I _____ shut it off.

4. If the sink is plugged up, he _____ use it.

5. If I need help, he _____ come over.

3 LESSON

Fire!

THINGS TO DO

1 Learn New Words 🎧

Look at the picture. Listen to the words. Then listen and repeat.

1. smoke
2. spray
3. fire escape
4. firefighter
5. fire truck
6. attach
7. hydrant
8. crawl
9. hose
10. ambulance
11. cover
12. ladder
13. climb up
14. climb down

Which words are new to you? Circle them.

2 Talk About the Picture

Write 5 things about the picture. Then share your ideas with the class.

EXAMPLE: One firefighter is climbing up the ladder.

3 Put in Order

Put the events in the story in order from first (1) to last (8).

___ He went to bed.

___ He called 911.

___ The smoke alarm in his bedroom went off.

___ The fire trucks arrived.

___ He smelled smoke.

_1_ Sam turned on the electric heater in his bedroom.

___ He woke up.

___ The heater overheated.

4 Read and Write

Read the article on page 137. Use your own ideas to complete the story. Answer these questions in your writing.

1. How did the fire start?
2. Who called 911?
3. Was anyone hurt?
4. How long did it take to put out the fire?

APARTMENT FIRE LEAVES 17 HOMELESS

A fire last night at 1420 South Main St. damaged six apartments, forcing residents to find new homes for the night. Firefighters think the fire started when a space heater

Weather Emergencies

THINGS TO DO

1 Learn New Words 🎧

Look at the pictures. Listen to the words. Then listen and repeat.

① wind   ⑤ snow   ⑨ hurricane

② hail   ⑥ lightning   ⑩ thunderstorm

③ rain   ⑦ sleet   ⑪ tornado

④ fog   ⑧ temperature

Which words are new to you? Circle them.

2 Read and Take Notes

Make a chart like this. Read the emergency procedures. Take notes in the chart.

EMERGENCY	THINGS YOU SHOULD DO	THINGS YOU SHOULDN'T DO
a tornado	go to the basement	stand near a window
a hurricane		
a thunderstorm		

3 Write

Describe an emergency that you or someone you know experienced. Then share your writing with the class.

> EXAMPLE: Several years ago, lightning hit my friend's house. She was home alone at the time. The lightning broke the light over her front door and came into the house through the telephone. No one was hurt but my friend had to buy a new telephone.

★ ★

 TRY THIS Use the Internet to learn more about storms. Find out if there are many hurricanes, thunderstorms, or tornados where you live. If so, find out when the season is for these storms so you can be prepared.

★ ★

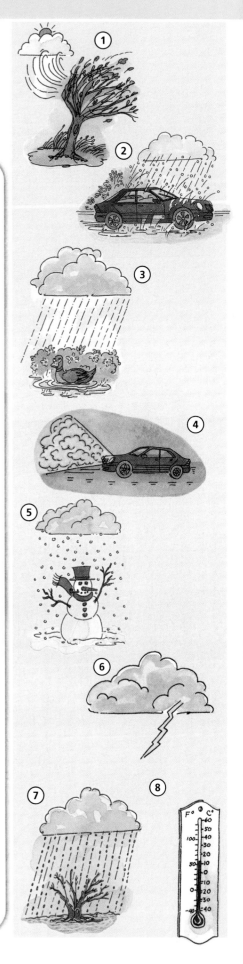

Emergency Procedures

HURRICANE

If there is a hurricane, it's important to:
- stay calm.
- stay indoors.
- stay away from windows and glass doors.
- protect windows with boards, shutters, or tape.
- keep tuned to radio reports.
- watch out for loose or dangling power lines.
- secure outdoor objects or bring them indoors.
- put gas in your car.
- save enough water to last for several days.

THUNDERSTORM

If there is a thunderstorm, it's important to:
- get into a building or a car.
- protect windows with boards, shutters, or tape.
- secure outdoor objects or bring them indoors.
- not handle any electrical equipment or telephones because lightning could follow the wire. Television sets are particularly dangerous at this time.
- keep tuned to a battery operated radio or television for the latest storm information.
- avoid bathtubs, water faucets, and sinks because metal pipes can transmit electricity.
- avoid tall structures such as towers, tall trees, fences, telephone lines, or power lines.
- stay away from rivers, lakes, or other bodies of water.

TORNADO

If there is a tornado, it's important to:
- stay away from all windows.
- go to the basement.
- if you don't have a basement, go to a small room without windows and get down on the floor.
- get under the stairs or a heavy table.
- protect your neck and head with your arms—lie down and cover your head.
- not try to out drive a tornado. Get out of the car immediately and find shelter in a nearby building.

WINDOW ON MATH
Converting Temperatures

 Read the information below.

To convert Fahrenheit (F) to Celsius (C), subtract 32, multiply by 5, and divide the result by 9.

> EXAMPLE: It's 50 degrees F. What is the temperature in Celsius? 50 – 32 = 18; 18 × 5 = 90; 90/9 = 10

To convert Celsius to Fahrenheit, multiply by 9, divide by 5, and add 32.

> EXAMPLE: It's 10 degrees C. What is the temperature in Fahrenheit? 10 × 9 = 90; 90/5 = 18; 18 + 32 = 50

 Convert these temperatures.

1. 32 ° F = _____ °C
2. 86 ° F = _____ °C
3. 40 °C = _____ ° F
4. 15 °C = _____ ° F

What's the weather forecast?

LESSON 5

1 Practice the Conversation: Talking About the Weather Forecast 🎧

Listen to the conversation. Then listen and repeat.

A: What's the weather forecast for this weekend?

B: It looks like hail on Saturday, and snow on Sunday.

A: That doesn't sound very good. Let's rent some movies and stay in .

B: Good idea.

Practice the conversation with a partner. Use these ideas.

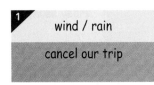

1 wind / rain

cancel our trip

2 fog / lightning

stay in and work on the kitchen

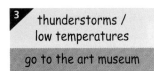

3 thunderstorms / low temperatures

go to the art museum

4

2 Practice the Conversation: Preparing for Bad Weather 🎧

Listen to the conversation. Then listen and repeat.

A: What are you doing?

B: I'm unplugging everything .

A: Why are you doing that?

B: Because they're predicting a thunderstorm .

A: Really? Did you unplug my computer ?

B: Yes, I did.

Practice the conversation with a partner.
Use these ideas.

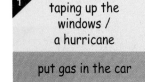

1 taping up the windows / a hurricane

put gas in the car

2 closing the sliding door / heavy rain

close the windows

3 bringing the chairs inside / heavy wind

hear the weather report on the radio

4

3 Listen and Write: Listening to a Weather Advisory 🎧

Listen to the weather advisory. Write the missing words. Then listen and check your answers.

This is Channel 5 news at 9:00 A.M. There is a weather advisory for the listening area today. Forecasters are

predicting _____ for the _____ . You are

advised to stay inside and away from _____ . We will bring you updated

information every _____ minutes.

WINDOW ON PRONUNCIATION 🎧
L versus *R* Sounds

 Listen to the pairs of words. Then listen and repeat.

1.	file	fire	4.	lamp	ramp
2.	wire	while	5.	list	wrist
3.	call	car	6.	right	light

 Listen to the pairs of sentences. Then listen and repeat.

1. It will be a wire.   It will be a while.

2. There's a file in the supply closet.   There's a fire in the supply closet.

3. Take a right.   Take a light.

 Work with a partner. Take turns reading each sentence and choosing a response.

> EXAMPLE: A: It will be a wire.
>   B: What color?

1. It will be a wire / while.

   A. What color?   B. How long?

2. There's a file / fire in the supply closet.

   A. Should I get it?   B. Did you call the fire department?

141

Home Hot Spots

1 Identify

Read the Fire Safety Tips below and study the picture on page 143. How many safety problems can you find in the picture?

EXAMPLE: The space heater is too close to the curtains.

DANGER ZONE	FIRE SAFETY TIPS
KITCHEN	Keep loose materials, such as dish towels and pot holders, away from the stove. Lock up matches and lighters so children cannot play with them. Never leave food on the stove, in the oven, or in the microwave unattended. Keep kids at least three feet away from a hot stove.
LIVING ROOM	Keep space heaters at least three feet away from rugs, walls, furniture, curtains, and other flammable materials. Never run electrical cords under rugs—the wires could fray and set the rug on fire. Also, don't overload electrical sockets with plugs.
BEDROOM	Don't fold electric blankets while they are plugged in. Never leave a lit candle unattended, and never smoke in bed.
BATHROOM	If an appliance is smoking or smells odd, unplug it immediately. Store flammable materials like nail polish, aerosol cans, towels, and magazines away from heated appliances like hair dryers.
BASEMENT, ATTIC, OR GARAGE	Keep flammable liquids, clothes, and papers away from the furnace, chemicals, and heat sources. Throw out oily rags, or store them in sealed containers.

2 Learn New Words

Read the words and their definitions.

overload = to put too many of something in one place   overflow = to flow or run over the top

overheat = to get too hot

Complete the sentences. Use a word from the list.

1. If you _____ the socket, it might cause a fire.

2. If the clothes dryer _____, it might burn your clothes.

3. If the toilet is plugged up, it might _____.

7 LESSON

What do you know?

1 Listening Review 🎧

Listen to the conversations. Choose the correct answer. Use the Answer Sheet.

1. A. That's okay.
   B. Yes, I did.
   C. No, I don't like lightning.

2. A. Turn on the television.
   B. Get more water.
   C. Get under the stairs or a table.

3. A. Yes, it's overheating.
   B. No, it's leaking.
   C. No, it's plugged up.

4. A. The firetrucks arrived.
   B. They put it out.
   C. A space heater overheated.

5. A. It's too hot.
   B. It's in the living room.
   C. It might overheat.

ANSWER SHEET

1	Ⓐ	Ⓑ	Ⓒ
2	Ⓐ	Ⓑ	Ⓒ
3	Ⓐ	Ⓑ	Ⓒ
4	Ⓐ	Ⓑ	Ⓒ
5	Ⓐ	Ⓑ	Ⓒ
6	Ⓐ	Ⓑ	Ⓒ
7	Ⓐ	Ⓑ	Ⓒ
8	Ⓐ	Ⓑ	Ⓒ
9	Ⓐ	Ⓑ	Ⓒ
10	Ⓐ	Ⓑ	Ⓒ

Listen and choose the best answer. Use the Answer Sheet.

6. A. Sure.
   B. How?
   C. How much?

7. A. The radio is in the kitchen.
   B. Okay.
   C. In the kitchen?

8. A. You should go to the basement.
   B. No, you shouldn't.
   C. Yes, you should.

9. A. 911
   B. the emergency room
   C. the radio report

10. A. smoke
    B. firefighters
    C. ladders

2 Dictation 🎧

Listen and write the sentences you hear.

1. _____

2. _____

3. _____

3 Conversation Check: Pair Work

Student A: Go to page 168.

Student B: Role play the conversations. Get information to complete this chart.

EXAMPLE: **B:** This is Keiko in apartment 7.
A: Yes, what can I do for you?
B: My kitchen faucet is leaking.

MAINTENANCE LOG				
Name	**Date**	**Time**	**Apartment**	**Problem**
Keiko	3/4	8:00 A.M.	7	kitchen faucet is leaking
David	3/4	10:15 P.M.	32	sink is plugged up
Maria	3/5	7:30 A.M.	18	bedroom window is stuck
Oscar	3/5	12 noon	26	
Sara	3/5	7:45 P.M.	17	roof is leaking
Jorge	3/6	11:30 A.M.	21	

How did you do? Check (✓) your answers.

✔

How many questions did you ask your partner?	How many questions did you answer?
□ 1 □ 2 □ 3	□ 1 □ 2 □ 3

✔ LEARNING LOG

I know these words:

□ ambulance	□ fire truck	□ ladder	□ sink	□ tornado
□ attach	□ firefighter	□ leak	□ sleet	□ turn down
□ bathtub	□ fog	□ lightning	□ sliding door	□ turn off
□ climb down	□ get plugged up	□ lock	□ smoke	□ turn on
□ climb up	□ get stuck	□ overheat	□ snow	□ unlock
□ clothes dryer	□ hail	□ pipe	□ space heater	□ unplug
□ cover	□ hair dryer	□ plug in	□ spray	□ wind
□ crawl	□ hose	□ put back	□ take out	
□ elevator	□ hurricane	□ rain	□ temperature	
□ faucet	□ hydrant	□ roof	□ thunderstorm	
□ fire escape	□ key	□ shut off	□ toilet	

I can ask:

□ Could you unplug the heater for me?
□ What can I do for you?
□ What's the weather forecast?

I can say:

□ I'll do it right away.
□ Don't unlock the door.
□ Turn off the lights.
□ They're predicting a thunderstorm.

I can write:

□ the ending of a story
□ a description of an emergency
□ notes about a reading
□ information on a maintenance request form

Spotlight: Grammar

FUTURE WITH *WILL*			
Statements	**Contractions**		
	Affirmative	*Negative*	
I He She **will be** there tomorrow. It **won't be** here tomorrow. You We won't = will not They	I'll he'll she'll it'll you'll we'll they'll	I won't he won't she won't it won't you won't we won't they won't	**Tip** Use *will* to make a promise, to offer help, or to make a prediction.

1 Complete the conversations with *will, 'll,* or *won't.*

1. A: Are you going to the party on Saturday?

    B: Yes, I am, but I _____ probably be late.

2. A: Are you going to be home early tonight?

    B: No, I _____. I have to work until 9:00.

3. A: Did you finish your homework?

    B: No, I didn't. I _____ finish it tomorrow.

4. A: Can we talk about this later?

    B: Sure. I _____ call you tonight.

5. A: Do you think Jean will go to the movies with us?

    B: No, I'm sure she _____.

6. A: Do you want to get together tomorrow?

    B: No, I can't. I think I _____ be at work all day.

7. A: Is your brother still sick?

    B: Yes, he is, but I think he _____ be better by tomorrow.

8. A: Is it going to rain tomorrow?

    B: I think so, but it _____ rain until the afternoon.

FUTURE CONDITIONAL STATEMENTS

- Conditional statements with *will* and *won't:*
  If it rains tomorrow, we **won't have** a picnic.
  If I stay up late tonight, **I'll feel** tired tomorrow.

- Conditional statements with *might* and *might not:*
  If you eat too much, you **might get** sick.
  If you don't study, you **might not pass** the test.

- Conditional statements with *should* and *shouldn't:*
  If it gets cold tonight, you **should turn up** the heat.
  If you feel sick tomorrow, you **shouldn't go** to work.

Tip

- Future conditional statements tell what will or might happen in the future under certain conditions.
  (condition)   (result)
- If she studies hard this week, she will pass the test.

- Use the simple present in the *if* clause.
  If I <u>feel</u> tired tomorrow, I might stay home.

- Use *will* to describe a definite future result. Use *might* to describe a possible future result. Use *should* to give advice.

2 Match each condition with a result.

Condition	Result
1. _____ If you call 911,	a. it won't work.
2. _____ If you lock the door,	b. you will hear about it on the radio.
3. _____ If you turn down the radio,	c. the smoke alarm will go off.
4. _____ If you use the elevator,	d. an ambulance will come right away.
5. _____ If the sink gets plugged up,	e. you won't bother the neighbors.
6. _____ If you crawl on the ground,	f. you will get dirty.
7. _____ If there is smoke in the house,	g. you won't get any exercise.
8. _____ If a hurricane is coming,	h. I won't be able to come in.

3 Complete these sentences with your own ideas.

1. If it rains tomorrow, I _____

2. If there is ever a hurricane here, I won't _____

3. If I feel sick tomorrow, I _____

4. If I need some money tomorrow, _____

5. If someone calls me up in the middle of the night, I _____

6. If the smoke alarm in my house goes off, I _____

7. If I lose my house key, I _____

8. If you have a problem with the electricity at home, you _____

She works with numbers.

THINGS TO DO

1 Learn New Words 🎧

Look at the pictures. Listen to the words. Then listen and repeat.

① computer programmer
② accountant
③ administrative assistant
④ dental assistant
⑤ caregiver
⑥ nursing assistant
⑦ assembler
⑧ machine operator
⑨ painter
⑩ electrician
⑪ bricklayer
⑫ welder

Which words are new to you? Circle them.

2 Write

Choose a job to complete each sentence. More than one answer may be possible.

1. _____An accountant_____ works with numbers.
2. _____ takes care of sick people.
3. _____ cleans teeth.
4. _____ fixes electrical problems.
5. _____ puts parts together.
6. _____ works with metal.
7. _____ takes phone messages.

3 Find Someone Who

Talk to different classmates. Find someone who answers yes to each question. Write the person's name.

A: Do you want to work in an office ?
B: Yes, I do. (or No, I don't.)

Find someone who_____.	Person's Name
wants to work in an office	_____
likes to work with numbers	_____
wants to work in health care	_____
wants to work outdoors	_____

Administration / Clerical

① ② ③

OCCUPATIONS

Building & Construction

⑫

⑪

Health Care

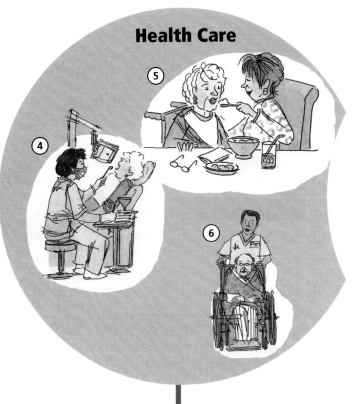

Manufacturing

OR JOBS

WINDOW ON GRAMMAR
Have to/Don't have to

A Read the sentences.

A bricklayer **has to be** strong.

An accountant **has to be** good with numbers.

A painter **doesn't have to be** tall.

B Complete the sentences. Use *has to* or *doesn't have to*.

1. A salesperson _____ talk to people.
2. An accountant _____ be a strong person.
3. A welder _____ be a man.
4. An electrician _____ have a license.
5. A teacher _____ have college degree.

2 LESSON

He works well with others.

THINGS TO DO

1 Learn New Words 🎧

Look at the pictures. Listen to the words. Then listen and repeat.

① **have computer skills**　　⑤ **work well with others**
② **have good people skills**　⑥ **work independently**
③ **be punctual**　　　　　　⑦ **solve problems**
④ **be dependable**　　　　　⑧ **follow directions**

Which words are new to you? Circle them.

2 Give Opinions

Complete the sentences. Write *has to* or *doesn't have to*.

1. A mechanic _____ have computer skills.
2. A painter _____ be dependable.
3. A bricklayer _____ solve problems.
4. An electrician _____ follow directions.
5. A doctor _____ be punctual.
6. A welder _____ have computer skills.

3 Evaluate

Rate yourself. Check (✓) your answers.

	Above Average	Average	Below Average
	*****	***	*
My computer skills are	☐	☐	☐
My people skills are	☐	☐	☐
My problem-solving skills are	☐	☐	☐
My ability to work with others is	☐	☐	☐
My ability to follow directions is	☐	☐	☐

Write about yourself.

My _____ skills are above average.

My ability to _____ is average.

★ ★

TRY THIS What are the people in your family good at? Write 5 sentences.

EXAMPLES: My sister, Anita, is good at solving problems.

My father is good at working with others.

★ ★

WINDOW ON GRAMMAR
Would like/Would rather

A Read the sentences.

I **would like to work** in health care someday.

I **wouldn't like to be** a dentist.

I **would rather be** a doctor than a dentist.

I**'d rather work** outside than inside.

B Complete the sentences with *would like to* or *wouldn't like* to.

1. I _____ take care of sick people.
2. I _____ be more punctual.
3. I _____ work with numbers.
4. I _____ answer phones.

C Work with a partner. Ask and answer the questions.

1. Would you rather be an electrician or a painter?
2. Would you rather be _____ or _____?

3
LESSON

I'd rather work full time.

Elisa

THINGS TO DO

1 Learn New Words 🎧

Look at the pictures. Listen to the words. Then listen and repeat.

① employment office   ⑤ file cabinet   ⑨ day shift
② conference room   ⑥ file folder   ⑩ evening shift
③ supply cabinet   ⑦ full time   ⑪ night shift
④ cubicle   ⑧ part time

Which words are new to you? Circle them.

2 Talk About the Picture

Write 5 things about the picture. Then share your ideas with the class.

> EXAMPLE: Mia is very organized.

3 Practice the Conversation 🎧

Listen to the conversation. Then listen and repeat.

A: Do you have any experience as a welder ?

B: Yes, I do. I worked as one in my country.

A: Are you good at working on a team ?

B: Yes, I am. I had to work on a team in my last job.

A: Would you rather work the day shift or the night shift ?

B: I prefer the day shift but I can work either one.

Practice the conversation with a partner. Use these ideas.

1 an accountant/working independently
work independently
full time or part time
full time

2 a nursing assistant/solving problems
solve problems
the evening shift or the night shift
the night shift

3 a machine operator/fixing things quickly
fix things quickly
days or evenings
evenings

4 a caregiver/following directions
follow directions
full time or part time
part time

LESSON 4

Starting a New Job

THINGS TO DO

1 Predict

Look at the pictures and read the title of the article. What do you think the article is about? Check (✓) your guess.

☐ things a nursing assistant does on the job

☐ things you should and shouldn't do at work

☐ things you should do to find a job

2 Read and Take Notes

Make a chart like this. What should and shouldn't you do on your first day at a new job? Read the article and list your answers in the chart.

SHOULD	SHOULDN'T
• dress appropriately	

3 Write

Write a story about someone's first day on the job. Read your story to the class. Let your classmates tell what the person did right and wrong.

EXAMPLE: On Nancy's first day of work she arrived early. She was introduced to many coworkers. She can't remember all their names. She ate lunch at her desk. She called her sister to tell her about the new job. She didn't have time to talk to her supervisor.

★ ★

TRY THIS Go to your local library. Ask the librarian where you can find resources for "job hunting." The library has a lot of resources to help you do well in interviews, write a good résumé, and find a new job.

★ ★

FIRST DAY ON THE JOB

It's important to make the right impression when you start a new job. Here are some tips to help you on your first day.

Dress appropriately

Before your first day, find out if your new job has a dress code (rule about what you can wear to work). If so, be sure to follow it. No matter what, always be neat and clean.

Get to work on time

Employers value employees who come to work on time. Give yourself an extra 15 minutes to make sure you arrive on time.

Pay attention to introductions

Your supervisor may introduce you to coworkers. These co-workers will be important to you. They will answer your questions when the boss is not around. Try to remember their names.

no matter what: in any situation

Ask plenty of questions

Make sure your supervisor tells you what she expects of you. Learn your job duties as soon as possible. Set goals for yourself.

Do not take too long for lunch

Find out about the lunch-hour policy at your new job. Ask if people eat at their desks or take a full hour outside the workplace. No matter what, never take longer than the time allowed.

Do not make personal telephone calls

You should never make personal phone calls to your friends and family unless it is an emergency.

WINDOW ON MATH
Overtime Pay

 Read the information below.

When an employee works more than 40 hours a week, each extra hour over 40 is overtime. Overtime pay is "time and a half." The employee gets the regular hourly pay plus one half the regular hourly rate.

EXAMPLE: Tom earns $10.00 an hour. If he works more than 40 hours, he should get $10.00 + $5.00, or $15.00, for each hour of overtime.

 Answer the word problems.

1. Jan earns $12.00 an hour. Last week she worked 46 hours. How much money did she earn?

2. Mr. Li earns $20.00 an hour. If he works 50 hours this week, how much will he earn?

5 LESSON

Are you willing to travel?

1 Practice the Conversation: Describing Skills and Experience 🎧

Listen to the conversation. Then listen and repeat.

A: Why are you applying for this position?
B: I enjoy working with people .
A: Are you willing to travel ?
B: Yes, I am. In my last job, I had to travel a lot.
A: Tell me about your experience with office work .
B: I worked as an administrative assistant for three years.

Practice the conversation with a partner.
Use these ideas.

1 working on a team	2 working with my hands	3 working independently	4
work long hours	work weekends	work the night shift	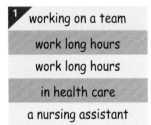
work long hours	work weekends	work the night shift	
in health care	in construction work	with electrical work	
a nursing assistant	a bricklayer	an electrician	

2 Practice the Conversation: Asking about Job Ads 🎧

Listen to the conversation. Then listen and repeat.

A: Did you say you were interested in the electrician's job?
B: Yes, that's right.
A: Do you have any questions about the job?
B: Yes. Is it a full-time job?
A: No, it's a part-time job .

Practice the conversation with a partner.
Use these ideas.

1 caregiver's	2 accountant's	3 mechanic's	4
Is it an evening job?	Is it a part-time job?	Is it for the day shift?	
a day job	a full-time job	for the night shift	

3 Practice the Conversation: Phoning in an Excuse 🎧

Listen to the conversation. Then listen and repeat.

A: Hello, is this Mr. Roberts?

B: Yes, it is.

A: This is Magda Perkins. I'm sorry, but
   I can't come in today. I'm really sick.

B: I hope you feel better.

A: Thank you.

Practice the conversation with a partner.
Use these ideas.

1 I'll be late this morning.
I had a car accident.

Oh, I'm sorry. We'll see
you later then.

2 I have to miss work tonight.
My daughter is in the hospital.

That's terrible. I hope
she's okay.

3 I can't work today.
I sprained my ankle.

That's too bad. Take it
easy.

4

WINDOW ON PRONUNCIATION 🎧
Intonation in *Yes/No* and *Wh-* Questions

A Listen to the questions. Then listen and repeat.

Rising intonation in *yes/no* questions	Drop-rise intonation in *Wh-* questions
Are you applying for this position?	Why are you applying for this position?
Did you work before?	Where did you work before?
Did you travel?	What did you do?
Did you supervise others?	How many people did you supervise?
Do you have any questions?	What questions do you have?

B Write 3 more questions of each type that an employer might ask in an interview.

Rising intonation in *yes/no* questions	Drop-rise intonation in *Wh-* questions
1.	1.
2.	2.
3.	3.

C Work with a partner. Role play a job interview. Ask and answer the questions.

157

Job Ads and Applications

1 Read and Identify

Tell about the jobs in the ads. Check (✓) your answers.

	JOB A	JOB B	JOB C	
1.	☐	☐	☐	is in health care.
2.	☐	☐	☐	pays well.
3.	☐	☐	☐	has night shifts available.
4.	☐	☐	☐	requires good people skills.
5.	☐	☐	☐	requires travel.
6.	☐	☐	☐	requires previous experience.

C

Service Technician
Service/repair equipment in textile manufacturing. Strong problem solving skills and electronic background a plus. Travel required. Good benefits and pay. Submit resume: J. Medford, P.O. Box 312, Harrisburg, PA.

A

Nursing Assistants Wanted
Needed for home care. Spanish-speaking CNAs needed for Hispanic cases. All shifts available. Great benefits. Must be punctual and good with people. Call ReLease Nurses at (601) 555-4800.

B

EXPERIENCED CONSTRUCTION WORKERS NEEDED

Painters, carpenters, bricklayers. Good pay. Travel required. Some long hours. Please contact Building Personnel at (336) 555-4670.

2 Read and Check *True* or *False*

Study the job application on page 159. Read the sentences below. Check (✓) *True* or *False*. Then correct the false sentences.

	True	False
1. Oscar Garcia has a high school diploma.	☐	☐
2. He studied to be a computer programmer.	☐	☐
3. He went to college for 3 years.	☐	☐
4. He would like to work full time.	☐	☐
5. He would rather work the 2nd shift.	☐	☐
6. At McHale Textiles, his starting salary was $9.00 an hour.	☐	☐
7. He supervises one person at McHale Textiles.	☐	☐
8. He worked at Gould before he worked at McHale.	☐	☐
9. He worked at Gould for more than a year.	☐	☐
10. He left Gould because he didn't like his supervisor.	☐	☐

APPLICATION FOR EMPLOYMENT

Last Name _Garcia_   First _Oscar_   Middle _Manuel_

Position Desired _Machine Operator_

Do you want to work: [X] Full time?   [ ] Part time?   What shift? [X] 1st [ ] 2nd [ ] 3rd

When will you be available to begin work? _in two weeks_

EDUCATION

School	Name and Location	Course of Study	Number of years completed	Did you graduate?	Degree or Diploma
College	Central Community College, Covina, California	Electronic technology	1.5	[X] yes [ ] no	Certificate in electronic technology
High	Covina High School, Covina, California	Tech course	4	[X] yes [ ] no	Diploma
Other	Cedar Adult Program Ontario, California	Auto mechanics	2	[ ] yes [X] no	NA

EMPLOYMENT   Please give complete full-time and part-time employment record. Start with present or most recent employer.

Company Name	Telephone
McHale Textiles	(703)555-9282

Address	Employed (Month and Year)
1320 West Avenue, Springfield, VA, 22151	From: 7/04 To: present

Name of Supervisor	Hourly Pay
Joe Lewis	Start: $12 Last: $12

State Job Title and Describe Your Work	Reason for leaving NA
Machine Operator/Team Leader. Monitor machinery, do quality checks, complete daily operating reports, supervise 5 people.	

Company Name	Telephone
Gould Technical Fabrics	(626)555-8776

Address	Employed (Month and Year)
467 Bates Parkway, Covina, CA, 91722	From: 2/02 To: 5/04

Name of Supervisor	Hourly Pay
Anthony Delaney	Start: $9 Last: $11

State Job Title and Describe Your Work	Reason for leaving
Machine Operator. Set up and operated machinery. Packaged and labeled products.	Company closed

What do you know?

LESSON 7

1 Listening Review 🎧

Listen to the conversations. Choose the job you hear. Use the Answer Sheet.

1. A.  B.  C.

2. A.   B.   C.

3. A.  B.   C.

4. A.  B.   C.

5. A.  B.   C.

ANSWER SHEET			
1	A	B	C
2	A	B	C
3	A	B	C
4	A	B	C
5	A	B	C
6	A	B	C
7	A	B	C
8	A	B	C
9	A	B	C
10	A	B	C

Listen to the conversations. Choose the correct response. Use the Answer Sheet.

6. A: Yes, I was a nursing assistant for two years.
B: Yes, thank you.
C: I don't know.

7. A: Yes, I would.
B: Days, I think.
C: Is that part time?

8. A: What time?
B: No, it's part time.
C: No, it's full time.

9. A: I'll be late today.
B: See you later.
C: I hope you feel better.

10. A: I did construction work for 2 years.
B: I was an administrative assistant for 2 years.
C: I was in health care for 2 years.

2 Conversation Check: Pair Work

Student A: Go to page 168.

Student B: Ask your partner questions to complete this chart.

EXAMPLE: **B:** How punctual is Rita?
A: Above average.

EMPLOYEE EVALUATIONS

	Employees	
	Rita Pons	Nick Walton
1. How punctual is the employee?	3	2
2. How well can the employee solve problems?		3
3. How well does he/she work on a team?	3	
4. How well does he/she follow directions?		2
5. How dependable is the employee?	1	

3 = ABOVE AVERAGE   2 = AVERAGE   1 = BELOW AVERAGE

✔

How many questions did you ask your partner?	How many questions did you answer?
☐ 1 ☐ 2 ☐ 3 ☐ 4 ☐ 5	☐ 1 ☐ 2 ☐ 3 ☐ 4 ☐ 5

✔ LEARNING LOG

I know these words:

- ☐ accountant
- ☐ administration
- ☐ administrative assistant
- ☐ assembler
- ☐ be dependable
- ☐ be punctual
- ☐ bricklayer
- ☐ building
- ☐ caregiver
- ☐ clerical
- ☐ computer programmer
- ☐ conference room
- ☐ construction
- ☐ cubicle
- ☐ day shift
- ☐ dental assistant
- ☐ electrician
- ☐ employment office
- ☐ evening shift
- ☐ file cabinet
- ☐ file folder
- ☐ follow directions
- ☐ full time
- ☐ have computer skills
- ☐ have good people skills
- ☐ health care
- ☐ machine operator
- ☐ manufacturing
- ☐ night shift
- ☐ no matter what
- ☐ nursing assistant
- ☐ painter
- ☐ part time
- ☐ solve problems
- ☐ supply cabinet
- ☐ welder
- ☐ work independently
- ☐ work well with others

I can ask:

- ☐ Would you rather be a doctor or a dentist?
- ☐ Is it a full-time job?
- ☐ Do you have experience as a welder?

I can say:

- ☐ I would like to work in health care someday.
- ☐ I'd rather be a doctor than a dentist.
- ☐ I prefer the day shift.
- ☐ I have experience as a . . .
- ☐ I enjoy working with people.
- ☐ I worked as a . . . for three years.
- ☐ I can't come in today.
- ☐ I'll be late this morning.

I can write:

- ☐ about my skills and abilities
- ☐ a list of job do's and dont's
- ☐ a short description of a day at work

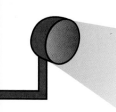

Spotlight: Writing

1 To apply for some jobs, you need to submit a résumé. Study the résumé and answer the questions below.

Elva Montoya

991 Houston St. • San Antonio, TX 78205 • (210) 555-9932 • elvarocks@hitmail.com

JOB OBJECTIVE: Position as administrative assistant

SUMMARY OF QUALIFICATIONS

- Excellent computer skills, familiar with Microsoft Office
- Good interpersonal skills, including the ability to work on a team and interact with customers or patients
- Bilingual

RELEVANT EXPERIENCE

- Four years experience as an administrative assistant in an accounting office
- Two years experience as a receptionist in a medical office
- 1.5 years as a teacher

WORK HISTORY

2001–present	**JG Accounting, San Antonio, TX** Admistrative assistant to firm partner
1998–2001	Full-time parent
1996–1998	**Antonio Medical** Receptionist
1994–1996	**Olinca School, Mexico City, Mexico** Math Teacher

EDUCATION

Accounting Technician Certificate, San Antonio College, San Antonio, TX, expected 2006

B.A. Universidad de Las Americas, Puebla, Mexico, graduated 1994

1. What job is Elva looking for? _____

2. What job does she have now? _____

3. What was her first job?_____

2 Put this person's jobs in order. Start with the most recent one.

◯ 1996–1998   **E.B. Electrics**
                Administrative Assistant

① 2003–present   **Pacific Electrical**
                Senior Electrician

◯ 1998–2000   **Garcia Electrical Services**
                Electrician's Assistant

◯ 2000–2003   **Northwest Electrical**
                Electrician

> **FOCUS ON WRITING:**
> Sequencing in a Résumé
>
> When we write a résumé, we often list our work history and education in reverse order. The most recent job and school come first.

3 Complete the résumé worksheet below.

Name and contact information: _____

JOB OBJECTIVE: _____

QUALIFICATIONS

• _____

• _____

EXPERIENCE

• _____

• _____

WORK HISTORY

(last or current job)

When _____ Where: _____

                     Job: _____

(job before your last job)

When _____ Where: _____

                     Job: _____

EDUCATION

What degree: _____ Where: _____ When: _____

Conversation Checks

1 UNIT   Conversation Check: Pair Work

Student A: Complete the questions below. Then ask your partner the questions and write his or her answers.

Questions

1. What _____ your last name? _____

2. What _____ your birthplace? _____

3. _____ you have a driver's license? _____

4. Do you _____ music? _____

How many questions did you ask your partner?	How many questions did you answer?
☐ 1 ☐ 2 ☐ 3 ☐ 4	☐ 1 ☐ 2 ☐ 3 ☐ 4

2 UNIT   Conversation Check: Pair Work

Student A: Ask your partner questions to complete the map.

EXAMPLE: **A:** What's behind the bank?
B: the medical center

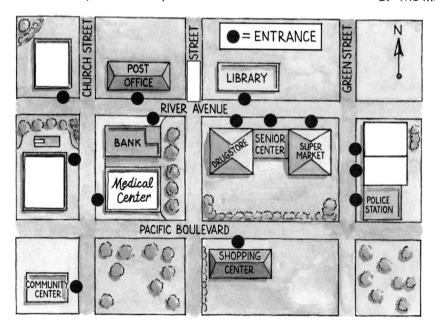

How many questions did you ask your partner?	How many questions did you answer?
☐ 1 ☐ 2 ☐ 3 ☐ 4 ☐ 5 ☐ 6	☐ 1 ☐ 2 ☐ 3 ☐ 4 ☐ 5 ☐ 6

Conversation Check: Pair Work

Student A: Ask your partner questions to complete this chart.

EXAMPLE: **A:** How much did Al spend on Tuesday?
B: Two dollars.

	Monday	Tuesday	Wednesday	Thursday
How much did Al spend?	$50.00	*$2.00*	$12.00	$225.00
What did he spend it on?				
How did he pay for it?				

How many questions did you ask your partner?	How many questions did you answer?
□1 □2 □3 □4 □5 □6	□1 □2 □3 □4 □5 □6

✔

Conversation Check: Pair Work

Student A: Ask your partner questions to complete this chart.

EXAMPLE: **A:** What are Sandy's academic goals?
B: She wants to graduate from college.

First Name	Personal	GOALS Academic	Work
1. Sandy	get married	*graduate from college*	start her own business
2. Michael		learn something new	
3. Latisha		learn more English	get a promotion
4. Mani	be a good citizen		
5. Zayda	become a U.S. citizen		

How many questions did you ask your partner?	How many questions did you answer?
□1 □2 □3 □4 □5 □6 □7 □8	□1 □2 □3 □4 □5 □6 □7

✔

165

Conversation Check: Pair Work

Student A: Ask your partner questions to complete this chart.

EXAMPLE: **A:** What's on sale at Lou's?
B: Blenders.
A: How much are they?
B: They're twenty percent off.

Lou's Discount House		Terry's Superstore	
What's on sale?	**How much?**	**What's on sale?**	**How much?**
blenders	20% off	vacuums	10% off
		coffeemakers	70% off
		mops	15% off
		can openers	half price

How many questions did you ask your partner?	How many questions did you answer?
☐1 ☐2 ☐3 ☐4 ☐5 ☐6 ☐7 ☐8	☐1 ☐2 ☐3 ☐4 ☐5 ☐6 ☐7 ☐8

Conversation Check: Pair Work

Student A: Ask your partner questions to complete this chart.

EXAMPLE: **A:** What did Sue have for an appetizer?
B: She had mushrooms.

Name	Appetizer	Main Dish	Dessert
Jane	XXXXXX	fish stew	a bowl of ice cream
Sue	mushrooms		
Tim	shrimp cocktail	a chicken sandwich	XXXXXX
Tom			

How many questions did you ask your partner?	How many questions did you answer?
☐1 ☐2 ☐3 ☐4 ☐5 ☐6	☐1 ☐2 ☐3 ☐4 ☐5 ☐6

Conversation Check: Pair Work

Student A: Ask your partner questions to complete this chart.

EXAMPLE: **A:** Who's Lana?
B: She's Rick's niece.
A: What's her occupation?

Name	John	Lana	Sam	Gino
Relationship to Rick	Rick's uncle	*Rick's niece*	Rick's neighbor	
Occupation				

✔

How many questions did you ask your partner?	How many questions did you answer?
☐ 1 ☐ 2 ☐ 3 ☐ 4	☐ 1 ☐ 2 ☐ 3 ☐ 4

Conversation Check: Pair Work

Student A: Ask your partner questions to complete this chart.

EXAMPLE: **A:** What's the matter with Mary?
B: She has a rash.
A: What did the doctor give her?

Name	What's the matter with him/her?	What did the doctor give him/her?
1. Chris		
2. Mary	*She has a rash.*	
3. Cynthia		
4. Alex		

✔

How many questions did you ask your partner?	How many questions did you answer?
☐ 1 ☐ 2 ☐ 3 ☐ 4	☐ 1 ☐ 2 ☐ 3 ☐ 4

Conversation Check: Pair Work

Student A: Roleplay the conversations. Get information to complete this chart.

EXAMPLE:
  A: This is Sara in apartment 17.
  B: Yes, what's the problem?
  A: My roof is leaking.

MAINTENANCE LOG				
Name	Date	Time	Apartment	Problem
Keiko	3/4	8:00 A.M.	7	*kitchen faucet is leaking*
David	3/4	10:15 P.M.	32	
Maria	3/5	7:30 A.M.	18	
Oscar	3/5	12 noon	26	clothes dryer is overheating
Sara	3/5	7:45 P.M.	17	roof is leaking
Jorge	3/6	11:30 A.M.	21	bathroom sink is plugged up

✔

How many questions did you ask your partner?	How many questions did you answer?
☐ 1 ☐ 2 ☐ 3	☐ 1 ☐ 2 ☐ 3

Conversation Check: Pair Work

Student A: Ask your partner questions to complete this chart.

EXAMPLE:
  A: How punctual is Nick?
  B: Average.

EMPLOYEE EVALUATIONS	Employees	
	Rita Pons	Nick Walton
1. How punctual is the employee?	3	2
2. How well can the employee solve problems?	2	
3. How well does he/she work on a team?		1
4. How well does he/she follow directions?	2	
5. How dependable is the employee?		2

3 = ABOVE AVERAGE   2 = AVERAGE   1 = BELOW AVERAGE

How many questions did you ask your partner?	How many questions did you answer?
☐ 1 ☐ 2 ☐ 3 ☐ 4 ☐ 5	☐ 1 ☐ 2 ☐ 3 ☐ 4 ☐ 5

A Nouns

Possessive Nouns

To form the possessive of any singular noun, add an apostrophe and -s.
Examples: John's book   Amy's map   the teacher's desk

To form the possessive of a plural noun that ends in -s, just add an apostrophe.
Examples: the boys' room   the girls' desks   the teachers' books

To form the possessive of a plural noun that does not end in -s, add an apostrophe and -s.
Examples: the men's room   the women's club   the children's teacher

Plural Nouns

To form the plural of:	Do this:	Examples:
most nouns	add -s	book—books student—students
most nouns that end in s, sh, ch, x, or z	add -es	address—addresses dish—dishes couch—couches box—boxes
most nouns that end in ay, ey, oy, or uy	add -s	day—days key—keys boy—boys
most nouns that end in f or fe	change the -f to -v and add -es or -s	wife—wives loaf—loaves
most nouns that end in a consonant and y	change the -y to -i and add -es	story—stories candy—candies penny—pennies family—families
most nouns that end in o	add -s	radio—radios shampoo—shampoos
some nouns that end in consonant and o	add -es	potato—potatoes

Capitalization

Capitalize the names of people.
Examples: Jan   T.S. Eliot   William Shakespeare

Capitalize geographical names.
Examples: Canada   New York   Main Street

Capitalize the names of organizations, holidays, religions, and languages.
Examples   New Year's Day   Islam   Spanish

Capitalize the days of the week and the months of the year.
Examples: Monday   Tuesday   Wednesday   January   February   March

B Adjectives

Possessive Adjectives

Here is	my your his her its	paper.		Here is	our your their	book.

Comparative Adjectives

Spelling Rules	Examples
One-Syllable Adjectives • Add *-er* to one-syllable adjectives. (If the adjective already ends in *-e,* add only *-r.*) • For one-syllable adjectives that end in a single vowel and a single consonant, double the consonant. Then add *-er.*	old—older cheap—cheaper large—larger hot—hotter sad—sadder
Two or More-Syllable Adjectives • For two-syllable adjectives that end in *-y,* change the *-y* to *-i* and add *-er.* • Use *more* with other adjectives that have two or more syllables.	pretty—prettier heavy—heavier peaceful—more peaceful important—more important
Irregular Adjectives • Some adjectives are irregular.	good—better bad—worse far—farther

Superlative Adjectives

Spelling Rules	Examples
One-Syllable Adjectives • Add *-est* to one-syllable adjectives. (If the adjective already ends in *-e,* add only *-st.*) • For one-syllable adjectives that end in a single vowel and a single consonant, double the consonant. Then add *-est.*	old—the oldest cheap—the cheapest large—the largest hot—the hottest sad—the saddest
Two or More-Syllable Adjectives • For two-syllable adjectives that end in *-y,* change the *-y* to *-i* and add *-est.* • Use *the most* with other adjectives that have two or more syllables.	pretty—the prettiest heavy—the heaviest peaceful—the most peaceful important—the most important
Irregular Adjectives Some adjectives are irregular.	good—the best bad—the worst far—the farthest

C Present Tense of *Be*

Affirmative Statements

I	am	a student.
You	are	a student.
He	is	a student.
She	is	a student.
It	is	a book.
We	are	students.
You	are	students.
They	are	students.

Negative Statements

I	am not	a teacher.
You	are not	a teacher.
He	is not	a teacher.
She	is not	a teacher.
It	is not	a map.
We	are not	teachers.
You	are not	teachers.
They	are not	teachers.

Contractions

I am	→	I'm		I am not	→	I'm not
you are	→	you're		you are not	→	you aren't/you're not
he is	→	he's		he is not	→	he isn't/he's not
she is	→	she's		she is not	→	she isn't/she's not
it is	→	it's		it is not	→	it isn't/it's not
we are	→	we're		we are not	→	we aren't/we're not
you are	→	you're		you are not	→	you aren't/you're not
they are	→	they're		they are not	→	they aren't/they're not

Yes/No Questions and Short Answers

Am	I			I	am.		I	'm not.
Are	you			you	are.		you	aren't.
Is	he			he	is.		he	isn't.
Is	she	late?	Yes,	she	is.	No,	she	isn't.
Is	it			it	is.		it	isn't.
Are	we			we	are.		we	aren't.
Are	you			you	are.		you	aren't.
Are	they			they	are.		they	aren't.

Information Questions

	am	I?
	are	you?
	is	he?
Where	is	she?
	is	it?
	are	we?
	are	they?

Who are you?	Why are you here?
Who is she?	Why is she here?
What is your name?	How are you?
What is her name?	How is she?
When is the party?	How old are you?
When are the holidays?	How old is she?

D Simple Present Tense

Affirmative Statements		
I	like	
You	like	
He	likes	
She	likes	music.
It	likes	
We	like	
You	like	
They	like	

Negative Statements		
I	don't like	
You	don't like	
He	doesn't like	
She	doesn't like	tea.
It	doesn't like	
We	don't like	
You	don't like	
They	don't like	

Yes/No Questions and Short Answers									
Do	I			I	do.		I	don't.
Do	you			you	do.		you	don't.
Does	he			he	does.		he	doesn't.
Does	she	like milk?	Yes,	she	does.	No,	she	doesn't.
Does	it			it	does.		it	doesn't.
Do	we			we	do.		we	don't.
Do	you			you	do.		you	don't.
Do	they			they	do.		they	don't.

Information Questions						
	do	I			Who do you live with?	Why do you smoke?
	do	you			Who does she live with?	Why does she smoke?
	does	he				
Where	does	she	live?		What do you like?	How do you do this?
	does	it			What does she like?	How does she do this?
	do	we				
	do	they			When do you get up?	How often do you eat?
					When does she get up?	How often does he eat?

E Present Continuous Tense

Affirmative Statements	
I	am working.
You	are working.
He	is working.
She	is working.
It	is working.
We	are working.
You	are working.
They	are working.

Negative Statements	
I	am not working.
You	aren't working.
He	isn't working.
She	isn't working.
It	isn't working.
We	aren't working.
You	aren't working.
They	aren't working.

Yes/No Questions and Short Answers

Am	I				I	am.		I	'm not.
Are	you				you	are.		you	aren't.
Is	he				he	is.		he	isn't.
Is	she	working?		Yes,	she	is.	No,	she	isn't.
Is	it				it	is.		it	isn't.
Are	we				we	are.		we	aren't.
Are	you				you	are.		you	aren't.
Are	they				they	are.		they	aren't.

Information Questions

	am	I		Who are you talking to?	Why are you leaving?
	are	you		Who is she talking to?	Why is she leaving?
	is	he			
What	is	she	doing?		
	is	it		Where are you working?	How are you feeling?
	are	we		Where is she working?	How is she feeling?
	are	they			

F Simple Past Tense

Affirmative Statements

I		
You		
He		
She	worked	yesterday.
It		
We		
You		
They		

Negative Statements

I		
You		
He		
She	didn't work	yesterday.
It		
We		
You		
They		

Yes/No Questions and Short Answers

	I				I			I	
	you				you			you	
	he				he			he	
Did	she	work yesterday?		Yes,	she	did.	No,	she	didn't.
	it				it			it	
	we				we			we	
	you				you			you	
	they				they			they	

Information Questions

Where	did	I you he she it we they	work?	Who did you work with? Who did she talk to?	Why did you go? Why did she leave?
				Who worked yesterday? Who called?	How did you get here? How did she feel?
				When did you arrive? When did she call?	What did you do? What did she say?

Past Tense of Irregular Verbs

bleed	bled	have	had	put	put
buy	bought	hurt	hurt	run	ran
come	came	is/are	was/were	see	saw
cost	cost	feel	felt	set	set
cut	cut	fry	fried	shut	shut
do	did	give	gave	sleep	slept
drink	drank	leave	left	spend	spent
eat	ate	make	made	take	took
get up	got up	meet	met		
go	went	pay	paid		

G Future Tense

Future with *Going to*

I	am going to			I	am not going to	
You	are going to			You	are not going to	
He	is going to			He	is not going to	
She	is going to	leave tomorrow.		She	is not going to	be here tomorrow.
It	is going to			It	is not going to	
We	are going to			We	are not going to	
You	are going to			You	are not going to	
They	are going to			They	are not going to	

Future with *Will*

I			I	
You			You	
He			He	
She	will come back soon.		She	won't be away for long.
It			It	
We			We	
You			You	
They			They	

won't = will not

H Modals

Might/Should				
I You He She It We You They	might leave early tomorrow. should be here tonight.		I You He She It We You They	might not leave until Wednesday. shouldn't be here on Thursday. shouldn't = should not

Have To/Don't Have To						
I	have to			I	don't have to	
You	have to			You	don't have to	
He	has to			He	doesn't have to	
She	has to	eat every day.		She	doesn't have to	eat out every day.
It	has to			It	doesn't have to	
We	have to			We	don't have to	
You	have to			You	don't have to	
They	have to			They	don't have to	

I Punctuation

Use a period (.) at the end of a sentence.
    Example: He isn't here.

Use a question mark (?) at the end of a question.
    Example: How are you?

Use a comma to separate things in dates and addresses.
    Examples: January 1, 2005
                  He lives in Sacramento, California.

ALL-STAR STUDENT BOOK 2 AUDIO SCRIPT

Note: This audio script offers support for many of the activities in the Student Book. When the words on the Student Book page are identical to those on the audio program, the script is not provided here.

PRE-UNIT

2. Complete the Conversations, page 2

Use a question or sentence from the box to complete the conversations. Then listen and check your answers.

1. A: What's your name?
   B: Keiko.
   A: How do you spell that?
   B: K-e-i-k-o.
2. A: Where are you from?
   B: I'm from Mexico. What about you?
   A: I'm from China.
3. A: What languages do you speak?
   B: Russian, French, and English.
   A: Really? That's interesting!
4. A: Do you like to watch flicks?
   B: I'm not sure. What is a flick?
   A: It's a movie.
   B: Then yes, I do.
5. A: Please turn to page 12.
   B: Could you repeat that?
   A: Please turn to page 12.
6. A: Would you be interested in studying tomorrow?
   B: I'm sorry. I don't understand your question.
   A: Do you want to study with me tomorrow?
   B: Yes, thank you.

3. Follow Instructions, page 3

Look at the pictures. Listen to the classroom instructions. Then listen and repeat.

1. Listen to the words.
2. Say, "Hello."
3. Write your name.
4. Sign your name.
5. Check (✓) *True* or *False*.
6. Take out a piece of paper.
7. Practice the conversation.
8. Raise your hand.
9. Underline the word.
10. Circle the word.
11. Hand in your homework.
12. Listen and repeat.

UNIT ONE

Lesson 1.

1. Learn New Words, page 4

Look at the pictures. Listen to the words. Then listen and repeat.

1. birth certificate	It's a birth certificate.
2. birthplace	His birthplace was Kingsville, Texas.
3. date of birth	His date of birth is March 2, 1975.
4. first name	His first name is Robert.
5. middle name	His middle name is Manuel.
6. last name	His last name is Garza.
7. sex	His sex is male.
8. driver's license	It's a driver's license.
9. address	His address is 1521 Market St.
10. hair color	His hair color is brown.
11. eye color	His eye color is brown.
12. height	His height is 5-10.
13. weight	His weight is 160 pounds.
14. diploma	It's a high school diploma.
15. signature	There's a signature on the diploma.
16. building pass	It's a building pass.
17. occupation	His occupation is nursing assistant.

Lesson 2.

1. Learn New Words, page 6

Look at the picture. Listen to the words. Then listen and repeat.

1. long hair	She has long hair.
2. short hair	He has short hair.
3. straight hair	He has straight hair.
4. curly hair	She has curly hair.
5. bald	He is bald.
6. beard	He has a beard.
7. mustache	He has a mustache.
8. tall	He is tall.
9. medium height	He is medium height.
10. short	He is short.
11. slim	She is slim.
12. heavy	He is heavy.
13. blond	Her hair is blond.
14. light brown	His hair is light brown.
15. dark brown	His hair is dark brown.
16. gray	His hair is gray.

Lesson 3.

2. Learn New Words, page 8

Look at the picture. Listen to the words. Then listen and repeat.

1. happy	He looks happy.
2. relaxed	He looks relaxed.
3. sad	She looks sad.
4. nervous	He looks nervous.
5. afraid	She is afraid.
6. bored	He looks bored.
7. angry	She looks angry.
8. tired	He looks tired.
9. radio	She has a radio.
10. slide	It's a slide.
11. swing	It's a swing.
12. basketball	He has a basketball.
13. camera	He has a camera.
14. toy	It's a toy.
15. laptop	He has a laptop.
16. cell phone	She has a cell phone.

Lesson 4.
1. Learn New Words, page 10
Look at the pictures. Listen to the words. Then listen and repeat.

1. music	She likes music.
2. swimming	She likes swimming.
3. loud noises	She doesn't like loud noises.
4. soccer	He likes soccer.
5. baseball	He doesn't like baseball.
6. housework	He doesn't like housework.
7. pets	He doesn't like pets.
8. motorcycles	He likes motorcycles.

Lesson 7.
1. Listening Review, page 16
Listen and choose the best answer. Use the Answer Sheet.

1. What color are his eyes?
2. What's Jon's date of birth?
3. Does he have a high school diploma?
4. What color hair does she have?
5. What's her address?
6. How's it going?
7. How are you doing?
8. Does she exercise every day?
9. Do you like to read?
10. Hi. My name is Robert.

2. Dictation, page 16
Listen and write the questions you hear. Then answer the questions.

1. What is your middle name?
2. Do you feel relaxed now?
3. Does your teacher have short hair?

UNIT TWO
Lesson 1.
1. Learn New Words, page 20
Look at the pictures. Listen to the words. Then listen and repeat.

1. study	She studies at the library every day.
2. check out books	They often check out books from the library.
3. buy stamps	I buy stamps at the post office.
4. mail letters	He mails letters at the post office.
5. mail packages	She mails packages at the post office.
6. get cash	He gets cash at the bank.
7. cash a check	I cash my check at the bank.
8. fill a prescription	You can fill a prescription at the drugstore.
9. buy medicine	We buy medicine at the drugstore.
10. buy groceries	He buys groceries at the supermarket.
11. see a doctor	They see a doctor at the medical center.
12. get a prescription	She gets a prescription from the doctor.

13. socialize	They socialize at the community center.
14. take classes	We take classes at the community center.
15. get something to drink	He often gets something to drink at a restaurant.
16. get something to eat	I often get something to eat at a restaurant.

Lesson 2.
1. Learn New Words, page 22
Listen to the words. Find the places on the map. Then listen and repeat.

1. between	The library is between the park and the drugstore.
2. next to	The police station is next to the community center.
3. across from	The post office is across from the police station.
4. avenue	The restaurant is on Central Avenue.
5. boulevard	The fire station is on Adams Boulevard.
6. on the corner of	The park is on the corner of Grove and Bristol.
7. block	The hotel and the shopping center are in the same block.
8. go north	Go north on Low Street.
9. go east	Go east on Adams Boulevard.
10. go south	Go south on Low Street.
11. go west	Go west on Adams Boulevard.
12. take a right	Take a right on Adams Boulevard.
13. take a left	Take a left on Scott Street.
14. go straight	Go straight on Diamond Street.

Lesson 3.
1. Learn New Words, page 24
Look at the picture. Listen to the words. Then listen and repeat.

1. ticket machine	Where is the ticket machine?
2. ticket office	Where's the ticket office?
3. platform	Where's the platform?
4. track	Where's the track?
5. snack bar	Where's the snack bar?
6. newsstand	Where's the newsstand?
7. information desk	Where's the information desk?
8. waiting area	Where's the waiting area?
9. baggage check	Where's the baggage check?
10. pay phone	Where's the pay phone?
11. buy a ticket	Who is buying a ticket?
12. wait for a train	Who is waiting for a train?
13. read a train schedule	Who is reading a train schedule?
14. make a phone call	Who is making a phone call?
15. in front of	Who is standing in front of Toby?
16. behind	Who is standing behind Hong?

ALL-STAR Student Book 2 Audio Script

Lesson 7.
1. Listening Review, page 32
Listen and choose the correct answer. Use the Answer Sheet.

1. How often do you go to the supermarket?
2. Where can you buy gasoline?
3. Where's the senior center?
4. What are they doing at the library?
5. How do I get to the community center?
6. Where can I get a train schedule?
7. When's the next train?
8. Is the train for Irvine on time?
9. How long does it take to get to Oceanside?
10. Where can I buy stamps?

UNIT THREE
Lesson 1.
1. Learn New Words, page 36
Look at the pictures. Listen to the words. Then listen and repeat.

1. groceries	How much do you spend on groceries?
2. recreation	How much do you spend on recreation?
3. toiletries	How much do you spend on toiletries?
4. bus fare	How much do you spend on bus fare?
5. car repairs	How much do you spend on car repairs?
6. car payments	How much do you spend on car payments?
7. rent	How much do you spend on rent?
8. utilities	How much do you spend on utilities?
9. gas	How much do you spend on gas?
10. electricity	How much do you spend on electricity?
11. cash	Do you pay your rent by cash?
12. credit card	Do you pay your rent by credit card?
13. personal check	Do you pay your rent by personal check?
14. money order	Do you pay your rent by money order?

Lesson 2.
1. Learn New Words, page 38
Look at the pictures. Listen to the words. Then listen and repeat.

1. toothbrush	Dana bought a toothbrush yesterday.
2. razor	Sam bought a razor yesterday.
3. shaving cream	Sam bought some shaving cream yesterday.
4. shampoo	Jim bought some shampoo yesterday.
5. toothpaste	Jim bought some toothpaste yesterday.
6. penny	Dana got a penny for change.
7. nickel	Dana got a nickel for change.
8. dime	Dana got a dime for change.
9. quarter	Dana got a quarter for change.
10. dollar	Dana got a dollar for change.
11. five dollars	Dana got five dollars for change.
12. ten dollars	Sam got ten dollars for change.
13. twenty dollars	Sam got twenty dollars for change.
14. fifty dollars	Sam gave the cashier fifty dollars.

Lesson 3.
1. Learn New Words, page 40
Look at the picture. Listen to the words. Then listen and repeat.

1. bank officer	The bank officer's name is Marie.
2. bank teller	Ali is a bank teller.
3. safe-deposit boxes	The safe-deposit boxes are near the exit.
4. ATM	There is an ATM at the front door of the bank.
5. check register	It's a check register.
6. checkbook	It's a checkbook.
7. deposit slip	It's a deposit slip.
8. withdrawal slip	It's a withdrawal slip.
9. savings account	She has a savings account.
10. ATM card	He has an ATM card.
11. monthly statement	It's a monthly statement.
12. paycheck	It's her paycheck.
13. endorse a check	You need to endorse a check to cash it.
14. make a deposit	He wants to make a deposit.
15. make a withdrawal	She wants to make a withdrawal.
16. open a checking account	He wants to open a checking account.

Lesson 4.
1. Learn New Words, page 42
Look at the pictures. Listen to the words. Then listen and repeat.

1. transaction amount	The transaction amount is $60.00.
2. balance	The balance is $385.89.

Lesson 4.
2. Read and Take Notes, page 42
Listen and check your work.

Check number: 326. Date: 9/16. Description: Veritas Telephone Company. Transaction amount: $42.76. Balance: $228.38.

Date: 9/17. Description: deposit. Deposit amount: $312.00. Balance: $540.38.

Check number: 327. Date: 9/18. Description: Bank Two. Transaction amount: $356.76. Balance: $183.62.

Date: 9/26. Description: Cash withdrawal. Transaction amount: $50.00. Balance: $133.62.

Date: 9/30. Description: deposit. Deposit amount: $850.00. Balance: $983.62.

Lesson 5.
1. Listen and Write: Listening to an Automated System, page 44
Listen and write the missing words. Then listen and check your answers.

Thank you for calling Horizon Bank. For existing account information, press 1. For all other services, press 2. To speak to a customer service specialist at any time, press 0.

For checking accounts, press 1. For savings, press 2. For credit cards, press 3.

Please enter you checking account number followed by the pound sign.

For personal accounts, please enter the last four digits of your social security number followed by the pound sign. Your available balance is $886.59.

Window on Pronunciation, page 45
C. Now listen again. You will hear one question from each pair in Activity B. Circle the correct answer.

1. What is that bang?
2. Do you have a sink?
3. Now think. What do you want?

Lesson 7.
1. Listening Review, page 48
Listen and choose the correct answer. Use the Answer Sheet.

1. How much do you spend on rent?
2. How do you pay for electricity?
3. Did you make a car payment last month?
4. Can you change a ten?
5. I'd like to make a deposit.
6. Who works in a bank?
7. What's the balance on your checking account?
8. How much is a quarter and two dimes?
9. How much is two twenties and a ten?
10. Do you have change for a ten?

2. Dictation, page 48
Listen and write the sentences you hear.

1. My friend bought some shampoo for two dollars and fifty cents.
2. She gave the store clerk five dollars.
3. The clerk gave her two dollars and fifty cents in change.

UNIT FOUR
Lesson 1.
1. Learn New Words, page 52
Look at the pictures. Listen to the words. Then listen and repeat.

1. become a U.S. citizen	He wants to become a U.S. citizen.
2. get married	They want to get married.
3. buy a house	She wants to buy a house.
4. be a good parent	She wants to be a good parent.
5. be a good citizen	He wants to be a good citizen.
6. get good grades	He wants to get good grades.
7. get vocational training	They want to get vocational training.
8. graduate from a university	She wants to graduate from a university.
9. get a GED	He wants to get a GED.
10. learn something new	She wants to learn something new.
11. get a job	He wants to get a job.
12. get a raise	She wants to get a raise.
13. get a promotion	He wants to get a promotion.
14. start a business	She wants to start a business.

Lesson 2.
1. Learn New Words, page 54
Look at the pictures. Listen to the words. Then listen and repeat.

1. go back to school	She wants to go back to school.
2. take a business course	She wants to take a business course.
3. save money	She wants to save money.
4. learn to use a computer	She wants to learn to use the computer.
5. take a writing course	She wants to take a writing course.
6. learn more English	He wants to learn more English.
7. vote	He votes.
8. do volunteer work	He does volunteer work.
9. read to your children	Do you read to your children?
10. spend time with your children	Do you spend time with your children?

Lesson 3.
1. Learn New Words, page 56
Look at the picture. Listen to the words. Then listen and repeat.

1. office manager	He is an office manager.
2. office worker	He is an office worker.
3. designer	He is a designer.
4. bookkeeper	She is a bookkeeper.
5. salesperson	He is a salesperson.
6. supervisor	He is a supervisor.
7. mechanic	She is a mechanic.
8. late	He is late.
9. on time	He is on time.
10. organized	She is organized.
11. disorganized	He is disorganized.
12. good with people	He is good with people.
13. hardworking	He is hardworking.
14. lazy	He is lazy.
15. bad attitude	He has a bad attitude.
16. good attitude	She has a good attitude.

Lesson 5.
3. Listen and Write: Listening to a Recorded Message, page 61
Listen and write the missing words. Then listen and check your answers.

Welcome to Westville Adult School. For information about Adult ESL classes, press 1. For information about vocational training, press 2. For information about computer classes, press 3. To register for next term, press 4. To hear this message again, press 5.

Lesson 7.
1. Listening Review, page 64
Listen to the conversations and choose the correct answer. Use the Answer Sheet.

1. I got a raise last week!
2. Sandra got married on Saturday.
3. I'm going to buy a house.
4. I am going to give you a raise.

Listen to the conversations and choose the correct answer. Use the Answer Sheet.

5. A: I'd like to register for a class.
   B: What would you like to take?
   A: A computer class.
   B: Here's the schedule.
   What class does he want?
6. A: How can I get a raise?
   B: You need to work here for at least three months.
   A: Anything else?
   B: Yes, do good work.
   What does she want?
7. This is Lee Valley Adult School. Please choose from the following options. For information about Adult ESL, press 1. For information about vocational training, press 2. To register for this term, press 3.
   What number should you press for ESL classes?

8. A: Did you have a good weekend?
   B: Yes, it was great. I went to the movies. How about you?
   A: I had fun too. I visited friends in Austin.
   What are they talking about?

Listen and choose the sentence with the same meaning. Use the Answer Sheet.

9. She got a better job at her company.
10. He's a good worker.

2. Dictation, page 64
Listen and write the sentences you hear.

1. Jon wants to get a promotion.
2. He went back to school.
3. He got the job as the new offfice manager.

UNIT FIVE
Lesson 1.
1. Learn New Words, page 68
Look at the pictures. Listen to the words. Then listen and repeat.

1. pair of athletic shoes	Do you have a pair of athletic shoes?
2. jacket	Do you have a jacket?
3. heavy coat	Do you have a heavy coat?
4. pair of boots	Do you have a pair of boots?
5. coffeemaker	Do you have a coffeemaker?
6. blender	Do you have a blender?
7. toaster	Do you have a toaster?
8. can opener	Do you have a can opener?
9. peeler	Do you have a peeler?
10. cutting board	Do you have a cutting board?
11. dish soap	Do you have any dish soap?
12. broom	Do you have a broom?
13. mop	Do you have a mop?
14. bucket	Do you have a bucket?
15. vacuum	Do you have a vacuum?

Lesson 2.
1. Learn New Words, page 70
Look at the picture. Listen to the words. Then listen and repeat.

1. carry	What is Jim carrying?
2. take a break	Who is taking a break?
3. go out of business	Which store is going out of business?
4. jewelry store	Where's the jewelry store?
5. go into	Which store is Carla going into?
6. toy store	Where's the toy store?
7. push a stroller	Who is pushing a stroller?
8. furniture store	Where's the furniture store?
9. sale	What's on sale at Arches Shoe Store?
10. demonstrate	What is Lola demonstrating?
11. mall directory	Where's the mall directory?
12. appliance store	Where's the appliance store?

Lesson 3.
1. Learn New Words, page 72
Look at the picture. Listen to the words. Then listen and repeat.

1. regular price	The regular price of the coffeemaker is $24.99.
2. 20 percent off	Ovay coffeemakers are now 20 percent off.
3. half price	All winter coats at Barb's Discount House are half price.
4. marked down 50 percent	Whirly vacuums are marked down 50 percent at Al's superstore.

Lesson 7.
1. Listening Review, page 80
Listen and choose the correct answer. Use the Answer Sheet.

1. Where did you get that stereo?
2. Which is cheaper—the coat or the jacket?
3. Did you buy anything yesterday?
4. When is the best time to buy electronics?
5. Are coffeemakers on sale?
6. Did you get a good deal on your vacuum?
7. Where can you buy a chair and table?
8. Why is May's Department Store better than Ben's?
9. What's Jim carrying?
10. What's on sale at Al's Department Store?

2. Dictation, page 80
Listen and write the sentences you hear.

1. What's the best place to buy shoes?
2. I like May's. It has the best sales.

UNIT SIX
Lesson 1.
1. Learn New Words, page 84
Look at the picture. Listen to the words. Then listen and repeat.

1. red meat	Did you eat any red meat yesterday?
2. poultry	Did you eat any poultry yesterday?
3. fish	Did you eat any fish yesterday?
4. eggs	Did you eat any eggs yesterday?
5. milk	Did you drink any milk yesterday?
6. ice cream	Did you eat any ice cream yesterday?
7. cheese	Did you eat any cheese yesterday?
8. oil	Did you have any oil yesterday?
9. fruit	Did you eat any fruit yesterday?
10. peanuts	Did you eat any peanuts yesterday?
11. vegetables	Did you eat any vegetables yesterday?
12. sugar	Did you have any sugar yesterday?
13. flour	Did you have any flour yesterday?
14. cereal	Did you eat any cereal yesterday?
15. soft drinks	Did you drink any soft drinks yesterday?
16. coffee	Did you drink any coffee yesterday?

Lesson 2.
1. Learn New Words, page 86
Look at the picture. Listen to the words. Then listen and repeat.

1. counter	They are sitting at the counter.
2. menu	She is looking at a menu.
3. waiter	The waiter is wearing a white shirt.
4. check	The waiter is giving her the check.
5. booth	They are sitting in a booth.
6. hostess	The hostess is seating them at a table.
7. tray	He is carrying a tray.
8. plate	There is a plate on the table.
9. bowl	There is a bowl on the table
10. napkin	There is a napkin on the table.
11. serve food	She is serving food.
12. take an order	She is taking an order.
13. pour	She is pouring water.
14. trip over	He tripped over a purse.
15. fall off	The glass is falling off his tray.
16. set the table	He is setting the table.
17. clear the table	She is clearing the table.
18. spill	He is spilling his milk.

Lesson 3.
1. Learn New Words, page 88
Look at the menu. Listen to the words. Then listen and repeat.

1. appetizers	What's your favorite appetizer?
2. soups	What's your favorite soup?
3. salads	What's your favorite salad?
4. main dishes	What's your favorite main dish?
5. sandwiches	What's your favorite sandwich?
6. side orders	What's your favorite side order?
7. desserts	What's your favorite dessert?
8. beverages	What's your favorite beverage?

Lesson 4.
1. Learn New Words, page 90
Look at the pictures. Listen to the words. Then listen and repeat.

1. fry	You can fry an egg.
2. bake	You bake bread.
3. boil	You boil water for tea.
4. cut up	You cut up vegetables to cook them.
5. slice	You can slice meat.
6. mix	You mix ingredients.
7. form a ball	You form a ball in your hand.
8. roll	You roll the ball in flour.
9. heat	You heat soup in a pan.

Lesson 5.
3. Listen and Write, page 93
Listen to 3 people ordering at a fast food restaurant. Check what each person orders. Then write the total you hear for each order.

1. A: Hi. I'd like a steak sandwich and a large root beer, please.
   B: OK. That will be $5.00.
2. A: Yes. I'd like a veggie sandwich, a small garden salad, and a small tea, please.
   B: Sure. That will be $5.25.
3. A: Hi. I'd like a chicken sandwich and a small orange soda.
   B: That will be $4.25.

Lesson 7.
1. Listening Review, page 96
Listen and choose the correct answer. Use the Answer Sheet.

1. Did you eat any meat or fish yesterday?
2. Did you have any fruit yesterday?
3. How much sugar does she put in her coffee?
4. Can you bring me a napkin, please?
5. Are you ready to order?
6. What's your favorite appetizer?
7. Do you want something to drink?
8. Can I get you something for dessert?
9. What's your favorite beverage in the morning?
10. How do you cook meatballs?

2. Dictation, page 96
Listen and write the sentences you hear.

1. Are you ready to order?
2. Yes. I'd like a large salad, please.
3. Do you want anything to drink?

UNIT SEVEN
Lesson 1.
1. Learn New Words, page 100
Look at the pictures. Listen to the words. Then listen and repeat.

1. grandparents — Manuel and Maria are Juan's grandparents.
2. parents — Tito and Rosa are Juan's parents.
3. aunt — Lupe is Juan's aunt.
4. uncle — Richard is Juan's uncle.
5. brother-in-law — Paul is Juan's brother-in-law.
6. nephew — Nick is Juan's nephew.
7. niece — Sofia is Juan's niece.
8. fiancée — Lisa is Juan's fiancée.
9. coworker — Tom is Juan's coworker.
10. boss — Mr. Li is Juan's boss.
11. friend — Joe is Juan's friend.
12. neighbors — Mrs. and Mr. Nath are Juan's neighbors.
13. landlady — Mrs. Chen is Juan's landlady.

Lesson 2.
1. Learn New Words, page 102
Look at the picture. Listen to the words. Then listen and repeat.

1. bride — Where's the bride?
2. groom — Where's the groom?
3. musicians — Where are the musicians?
4. photographer — Where's the photographer?
5. gifts — Where are the gifts?
6. in a bad mood — Who is in a bad mood?
7. kiss — Who is kissing Marta?
8. make a toast — Who is making a toast?
9. in a good mood — Who is in a good mood?
10. shake hands — Who is Ted shaking hands with?
11. hug — Who is Joe hugging?
12. dance — Who is dancing?

Lesson 3.
1. Learn New Words, page 104
Look at the pictures. Listen to the words. Then listen and repeat.

1. ask for advice — He's asking her for advice.
2. take care of — She's taking care of her grandmother.
3. compliment — He's complimenting her work.
4. apologize — He's apologizing.
5. disagree — They disagree about the food.
6. yell at — He yelled at the man to slow down.
7. criticize — He criticized the painter's work.
8. talk back — The boy talked back to his mother.

Lesson 6.
1. Learn New Words, page 110
Listen to the words for items you can mail. Then listen and repeat.

1. postcard — A postcard is not in an envelope.
2. letter — A letter is small and rectangular.
3. large envelope — A large envelope is no thicker than 3/4 inch.
4. package — A package weighs up to 70 pounds.

Lesson 7.
1. Listening Review, page 112
Listen to the conversations. Choose the best answer. Use the Answer Sheet.

1. A: I'm sorry I missed the party.
   B: That's okay. Another time.
2. A: Can I do anything for you?
   B: No, thanks. Everything is ready.
3. A: Ann, I want you to know I'm unhappy with your work.
   B: Am I disorganized?
   A: No, you're organized, but you're working much too slowly.
4. A: Did you have a good day at work?
   B: Well, yes and no.

A: What do you mean?
B: I got to work late and the boss got a little angry.
A: That's not good.
B: I know. What do you think I should do?
A: Maybe you should get to work very early tomorrow.
B: That's a good idea.
5. A: Who cleaned the kitchen last night?
B: I did.
A: Well, you did a really great job.
B: I'm glad you think so.

Lesson 7.
2. Listen and Write, page 112
Who are the people in the picture? Listen first. Then complete the sentences. Then listen again and check your answers.

This is a picture of my family. I'm the person in the middle. I'm wearing a blue shirt. The man next to me is my uncle. The woman next to me is my aunt. The man behind me is my brother-in-law and the boy in front of me is my nephew, standing next to his sister.

UNIT EIGHT
Lesson 1.
1. Learn New Words, page 116
Look at the pictures. Listen to the words. Then listen and repeat.

1. brain	It's a brain.
2. tooth	It's a tooth.
3. muscle	It's a muscle.
4. waist	It's a waist.
5. hip	It's a hip.
6. joint	It's a joint.
7. bone	It's a bone.
8. skin	It's skin.
9. blood	It's blood.
10. heart	It's a heart.
11. lungs	They're lungs.
12. back	It's a back.

Lesson 2.
1. Learn New Words, page 118
Look at the pictures. List to the words. Then listen and repeat.

1. burn	It's a bad burn.
2. cut	It's a deep cut.
3. fracture	It's a bad fracture.
4. sprain	It's a sprain.
5. bruise	It's a bruise.
6. shock	He got a shock from the electric cord.
7. rash	She has a rash on her leg.
8. fever	She has a fever.
9. cold	He has a cold.
10. flu	She has the flu.
11. infection	She has an infection on her finger.

12. feel dizzy	He feels dizzy.
13. blister	He has a blister on his hand.
14. feel nauseous	She feels nauseous.
15. bleed	The cut on his hand is bleeding.

Lesson 3.
1. Learn New Words, page 120
Look at the picture. Listen to the words. Then listen and repeat.

1. emergency room	Where's the emergency room?
2. examining room	Where's the examining room?
3. x-ray	He got an x-ray.
4. radiology	Where's the radiology department?
5. stitches	She got stitches.
6. sling	He has a sling.
7. ice pack	He has an ice pack.
8. admissions desk	Where's the admissions desk?
9. splint	He has a splint.
10. wheelchair	He's in a wheelchair.
11. waiting room	Where's the waiting room?
12. crutches	She has crutches.
13. cast	She has a cast.
14. bandage	She has a bandage.

Lesson 4.
1. Learn New Words, page 122
Look at the medicine labels. Listen to the words. Then listen and repeat.

1. tablet	Take two tablets.
2. teaspoon	Take two teaspoons.
3. cream	Use the cream two times a day.
4. OTC	The medicine is OTC.
5. capsule	Take two capsules.

Lesson 5.
Window on Pronunciation, page 125
Can Versus Can't
B. Listen to the sentences. Underline the word you hear.
1. He can't come to school today.
2. She can go back to work.
3. They can hear the teacher.
4. I can't exercise today.

Lesson 7.
1. Listening Review, page 128
Listen and choose the best answer. Use the Answer Sheet.
1. Take two tablets of this medicine three times a day.
2. Use this sling for two weeks.
3. You should keep this out of the reach of children.
4. I feel nauseous.
5. How did you injure your shoulder?
6. What did you sprain?
7. You may have a fracture.
8. You look terrible. What's the matter?
9. Did you hurt your ankle?
10. What happened to your leg?

2. Dictation, page 128
Listen and write the sentences you hear.
1. If you have a toothache, you should go to the dentist.
2. Is your rash getting any better?
3. Did you go to the emergency room?

UNIT NINE
Lesson 1.
Learn New Words, page 132
Look at the pictures. Listen to the words. Then listen and repeat.

1. shut off	Shut off the alarm clock.
2. plug in	Plug in the coffeepot.
3. take out	Take out the milk.
4. turn on	Turn on the radio.
5. turn off	Turn off the radio.
6. put back	Put back the milk.
7. turn down	Turn down the heat.
8. lock	Lock the door.
9. unlock	Unlock the door.
10. unplug	Unplug the coffeepot.

Lesson 2.
1. Learn New Words, page 134
Look at the picture. Listen to the words. Then listen and repeat.

1. leak	A faucet can leak.
2. faucet	The faucet is leaking.
3. pipe	The pipe is leaking.
4. roof	The roof is leaking.
5. overheat	A toaster oven can overheat.
6. space heater	The space heater is overheating.
7. clothes dryer	The clothes dryer is overheating.
8. hair dryer	The hair dryer is overheating.
9. get plugged up	A pipe can get plugged up.
10. sink	The sink is plugged up.
11. toilet	The toilet is plugged up.
12. bathtub	The bathtub is plugged up.
13. get stuck	A window can get stuck.
14. key	The key is stuck.
15. elevator	The elevator is stuck.
16. sliding door	The sliding door is stuck.

Lesson 3.
1. Learn New Words, page 136
Look at the picture. Listen to the words. Then listen and repeat.

1. smoke	There's a lot of smoke.
2. spray	They spray water on the fire.
3. fire escape	They are going down the fire escape.
4. firefighter	The firefighter is spraying water.
5. fire truck	The fire truck is next to the building.
6. attach	The firefighter needs to attach the hose.
7. hydrant	The firefighter attaches the hose to the hydrant.
8. crawl	The man crawls under the smoke.
9. hose	The hose brings water to the fire.
10. ambulance	The ambulance is in front of the building.
11. cover	The woman covers her mouth.
12. ladder	The firefighter is on the ladder.
13. climb up	The firefighter climbs up the ladder.
14. climb down	The man climbs down the ladder.

Lesson 4.
1. Learn New Words, page 138
Look at the pictures. Listen to the words. Then listen and repeat.

1. wind	There's a lot of wind today.
2. hail	There's a lot of hail today.
3. rain	There's a lot of rain today.
4. fog	There's a lot of fog today.
5. snow	There's a lot of snow today.
6. lightning	There's a lot of lightning today.
7. sleet	There's a lot of sleet today.
8. temperature	The temperature is low today.
9. hurricane	There may be a hurricane today.
10. thunderstorm	There may be a thunderstorm today.
11. tornado	There may be a tornado today.

Lesson 5.
3. Listen and Write: Listening to a Weather Advisory, page 141
Listen to the weather advisory. Write the missing words. Then listen and check your answers.

This is Channel 5 news at 9:00 A.M. There is a weather advisory for the listening area today. Forecasters are predicting thunderstorms for the weekend. You are advised to stay inside and away from windows. We will bring you updated information every twenty minutes.

Lesson 7.
1. Listening Review, page 144
Listen to the conversations. Choose the correct answer. Use the Answer Sheet.

1. A: What's the weather forecast for tonight?
   B: There's going to be a thunderstorm.
   A: Really? Did you unplug everything?

2. A: They're predicting a hurricane.
   B: Really? What should we do?

3. A: Hi. This is your tenant in apartment 123.
   B: Hi. What can I do for you?
   A: Could you look at my kitchen sink?
   B: Is it leaking again?

4. A: What happened last night?
   B: There was a fire on Main Street.
   A: Really? How did it start?

5. A: Did you unplug the space heater?
   B: No, I didn't.
   A: Could you do it for me?

B: Sure. Where is it?

Listen and choose the best answer. Use the Answer Sheet.

6. Would you please put the food away?
7. Could you please shut off the radio?
8. Should you go inside during a thunderstorm?
9. Where do you call to report a fire?
10. Who puts out fires?

2. Dictation, page 144
Listen and write the sentences you hear.

1. Could you turn off the lights, please?
2. The smoke alarm in his bedroom went off.
3. They are predicting rain for this weekend.

UNIT TEN
Lesson 1.
1. Learn New Words, page 148
Look at the pictures. Listen to the words. Then listen and repeat.

1. computer programmer	He is a computer programmer.
2. accountant	She is an accountant.
3. administrative assistant	She is an administrative assistant.
4. dental assistant	She is a dental assistant.
5. caregiver	She is a caregiver.
6. nursing assistant	He is a nursing assistant.
7. assembler	She is an assembler.
8. machine operator	He is a machine operator.
9. painter	He is a painter.
10. electrician	He is an electrician.
11. bricklayer	She is a bricklayer.
12. welder	He is a welder.

Lesson 2.
1. Learn New Words, page 150
Look at the pictures. Listen to the words. Then listen and repeat.

1. have computer skills	He has computer skills.
2. have good people skills	He has good people skills.
3. be punctual	He is punctual.
4. be dependable	He is dependable.
5. work well with others	He works well with others.
6. work independently	She works independently.
7. solve problems	He solves problems.
8. follow directions	He follows directions.

Lesson 3.
1. Learn New Words, page 152
Look at the pictures. Listen to the words. Then listen and repeat.

1. employment office	Where's the employment office?
2. conference room	Where's the conference room?
3. supply cabinet	Where's the supply cabinet?
4. cubicle	Where's her cubicle?
5. file cabinet	Where's the file cabinet?
6. file folder	Where's the file folder?

7. full time	Do you work full time?
8. part time	Do you work part time?
9. day shift	Do you work the day shift?
10. evening shift	Do you work the evening shift?
11. night shift	Do you work the night shift?

Lesson 7.
1. Listening Review, page 160
Listen to the conversations. Choose the job you hear. Use the Answer Sheet.

1. A: What does your brother do?
   B: He's a nursing assistant.
   A: Wow! A nursing assistant! That's great.
   B: Yes, he really likes it.

2. A: What did you do before you came here?
   B: I was a welder.
   A: How long did you work as a welder?
   B: For three years.

3. A: Would you like to be a dental assistant?
   B: No, I don't think so.
   A: Why not?
   B: I don't like to look in people's mouths.

4. A: Where does your brother work?
   B: At Farfield Manufacturing.
   A: What does he do there?
   B: He's a computer programmer.

5. A: Do you have any experience as a machine operator?
   B: Yes, I do. I worked as a machine operator in my country.
   A: That's great.

Listen to the conversations. Choose the correct response. Use the Answer Sheet.

6. A: Why are you applying for this job?
   B: I like working with people.
   A: Do you have any experience in health care?

7. A: I see you want a full-time position.
   B: Yes, that's right.
   A: Would you prefer to work days or evenings?

8. A: I have a question about the schedule.
   B: Okay. What's your question?
   A: Is it is a full-time job?

9. A: Hello, is this Ms. Smith?
   B: Yes, it is.
   A: This is Carlos. I can't come to work today. I'm really sick.

10. A: Are you willing to travel?
    B: Yes, I am. In my last job, I had to travel a lot.
    A: Tell me about your experience with office work.

VOCABULARY LIST

Numbers in parentheses indicate unit numbers.

accountant (10)
across from (2)
address (1)
administration (10)
administrative assistant (10)
afraid (1)
ambulance (9)
angry (1)
apologize (7)
appetizer (6)
appliance store (5)
ask for advice (7)
assembler (10)
ATM (3)
ATM card (3)
attach (9)
aunt (7)
avenue (2)
back (8)
bad attitude (4)
baggage check (2)
bake (6)
balance (3)
bald (1)
bandage (8)
bank officer (3)
bank teller (3)
baseball (1)
basketball (1)
bathtub (9)
be a good citizen (4)
be a good parent (4)
be dependable (10)
be punctual (10)
beard (1)
become a U.S. citizen (4)
behind (2)
between (2)
beverage (6)
birth certificate (1)
birthplace (1)
bleed (8)
blender (5)
blister (8)
block (2)
blond (1)
blood (8)
boil (6)
bone (8)
bookkeeper (4)
booth (6)
bored (1)
boss (7)
bother (7)
boulevard (2)
bowl (6)
brain (8)
bricklayer (10)
bride (7)
broom (5)
brother-in-law (7)
bruise (8)

bucket (5)
building (10)
building pass (1)
burn (8)
bus fare (3)
buy a house (4)
buy a ticket (2)
buy groceries (2)
buy medicine (2)
buy stamps (2)
camera (1)
can opener (5)
capsule (8)
car payments (3)
car repairs (3)
caregiver (10)
carry (5)
cash (3)
cash a check (2)
cast (8)
cell phone (1)
cereal (6)
check (6)
check out books (2)
check register (3)
checkbook (3)
cheese (6)
clear the table (6)
clerical (10)
climb down (9)
climb up (9)
clothes dryer (9)
coffee (6)
coffee maker (5)
cold (8)
compliment (7)
computer programmer (10)
conference room (10)
construction (10)
counter (6)
cover (9)
coworker (7)
crawl (9)
cream (8)
credit card (3)
criticize (7)
crutches (8)
cubicle (10)
curly hair (1)
custom (7)
customary (7)
cut (8)
cut up (6)
cutting board (5)
dance (7)
dark brown (1)
date of birth (1)
day shift (10)
deal with (7)
deduct (3)
demonstrate (5)
dental assistant (10)

deposit slip (3)
designer (4)
dessert (6)
dime (10c) (3)
diploma (1)
disagree (7)
dish soap (5)
disorganized (4)
do volunteer work (4)
dress up (7)
driver's license (1)
eggs (6)
elder (7)
elderly (7)
electrician (10)
electricity (3)
elevator (9)
emergency room (8)
employee (3)
employment office (10)
endorse a check (3)
evening shift (10)
examining room (8)
eye color (1)
fall off (6)
family affair (7)
faucet (9)
feel dizzy (8)
feel nauseous (8)
fever (8)
fiancée (7)
fifty dollars ($50.00) (3)
file cabinet (10)
file folder (10)
fill a prescription (2)
fire escape (9)
fire truck (9)
firefighter (9)
first name (1)
fish (6)
five dollars ($5.00) (3)
flour (6)
flu (8)
fog (9)
follow directions (10)
form a ball (6)
fracture (8)
friend (7)
fruit (6)
fry (6)
full time (10)
furniture store (5)
gas (3)
get a GED (4)
get a job (4)
get a prescription (2)
get a promotion (4)
get a raise (4)
get cash (2)
get good grades (4)
get married (4)
get plugged up (9)
get something to drink (2)

get something to eat (2)
get stuck (9)
get vocational training (4)
gifts (7)
go back to school (4)
go east (2)
go into (5)
go north (2)
go out of business (5)
go south (2)
go straight (2)
go west (2)
good attitude (4)
good with people (4)
graduate from a university (4)
grandparents (7)
gray (1)
groceries (3)
groom (7)
grow up (7)
hail (9)
hair color (1)
hair dryer (9)
half price (5)
happy (1)
hardworking (4)
have computer skills (10)
have good people skills (10)
healthcare (10)
heart (8)
heat (6)
heavy (1)
heavy coat (5)
height (1)
hip (8)
hose (9)
hostess (6)
housework (1)
hug (7)
hurricane (9)
hydrant (9)
ice cream (6)
ice pack (8)
in a bad mood (7)
in a good mood (7)
in front of (2)
infection (8)
information desk (2)
invitation (7)
jacket (5)
jewelry store (5)
joint (8)
key (9)
kiss (7)
ladder (9)
landlady (7)
laptop (1)
last name (1)
late (4)
lazy (4)
leak (9)

186

learn more English (4)
learn something new (4)
learn to use a computer (4)
light brown (1)
lightning (9)
lock (9)
long hair (1)
loud noises (1)
lungs (8)
machine operator (10)
mail letters (2)
mail packages (2)
main dish (6)
make a deposit (3)
make a phone call (2)
make a toast (7)
make a withdrawal (3)
mall directory (5)
manufacturing (10)
marked down (5)
mechanic (4)
medium height (1)
menu (6)
middle name (1)
milk (6)
mix (6)
money order (3)
monthly statement (3)
mop (5)
motorcycle (1)
muscle (8)
music (1)
musicians (7)
mustache (1)
napkin (6)
neighbors (7)
nephew (7)
nervous (1)
newsstand (2)
next to (2)
nickel (5c) (3)
niece (7)
night shift (10)
no matter what (10)
nursing assistant (10)
occupation (1)
office manager (4)
office worker (4)
oil (6)
on the corner of (2)
on time (4)
one dollar ($1.00) (3)
one way (2)
open a checking account (3)
organized (4)
OTC (8)
overheat (9)
package (7)
painter (10)
pair of athletic shoes (5)
pair of boots (5)
parents (7)

part time (10)
pay phone (2)
paycheck (3)
peanuts (6)
peeler (5)
penny (1c) (3)
personal check (3)
pets (1)
photographer (7)
pipe (9)
plate (6)
platform (2)
plug in (9)
postcard (7)
poultry (6)
pour (6)
problem (7)
problematic (7)
push a stroller (5)
put back (9)
quarter (25c) (3)
radio (1)
radiology (8)
rain (9)
raised on (7)
rash (8)
razor (3)
read a train schedule (2)
read to your children (4)
recreation (3)
red meat (6)
regular price (5)
relaxed (1)
religion (7)
religious (7)
rent (3)
respect (7)
respectful (7)
roll (6)
roof (9)
round trip (2)
sad (1)
safe-deposit box (3)
salad (6)
salary (3)
sale (5)
salesperson (4)
sandwich (6)
save money (4)
savings account (3)
see a doctor (2)
senator (4)
serve food (6)
set the table (6)
sex (1)
shake hands (7)
shampoo (3)
shaving cream (3)
shock (8)
short (1)
short hair (1)
shut off (9)
side order (6)

signature (1)
sink (9)
skin (8)
sleet (9)
slice (6)
slide (1)
sliding door (9)
slim (1)
sling (8)
smoke (9)
snack bar (2)
snow (9)
soccer (1)
socialize (2)
soft drink (6)
solve problems (10)
soup (6)
space heater (9)
spend time with your children (4)
spill (6)
splint (8)
sprain (8)
spray (9)
start a business (4)
stitches (8)
straight hair (1)
study (2)
sugar (6)
supervisor (4)
supply cabinet (10)
swimming (1)
swing (1)
tablet (8)
take a break (5)
take a business course (4)
take a left (2)
take a right (2)
take a writing course (4)
take an order (6)
take care of (7)
take classes (2)
take out (9)
talk back (7)
tall (1)
teaspoon (8)
teeth (8)
temperature (9)
ten dollars ($10.00) (3)
thunderstorm (9)
ticket machine (2)
ticket office (2)
tired (1)
toaster (5)
toilet (9)
toiletries (3)
tooth (8)
toothbrush (3)
toothpaste (3)
tornado (9)
toy (1)
toy store (5)
track (2)

tradition (7)
traditional (7)
transaction amount (3)
tray (6)
trip over (6)
turn down (9)
turn down (7)
turn off (9)
turn on (9)
twenty dollars ($20.00) (3)
twenty percent off (5)
uncle (7)
unlock (9)
unplug (9)
utilities (3)
vacuum (5)
vegetable (6)
vote (4)
waist (8)
wait for a train (2)
waiter (6)
waiting area (2)
waiting room (8)
weight (1)
welder (10)
wheelchair (8)
wind (9)
withdrawal slip (3)
work independently (10)
work well with others (10)
x-ray (8)
yell at (7)

SKILLS INDEX

Skills Index